The Visual Dictionary of Architecture

An AVA Book
Published by AVA Publishing SA
Rue des Fontenailles 16
Case Postale
1000 Lausanne 6
Switzerland
Tel: +41 786 005 109
Email: enquiries@avabooks.ch

Distributed by Thames & Hudson (ex-North America)
181a High Holborn
London WC1V 7QX
United Kingdom
Tel: +44 20 7845 5000
Fax: +44 20 7845 5055
Email: sales@thameshudson.co.uk
www.thamesandhudson.com

Distributed in the USA & Canada by
Watson-Guptill Publications
770 Broadway
New York, New York 10003
USA
Fax: 1-646-654-5487
Email: info@watsonguptill.com
www.watsonguptill.com

English Language Support Office
AVA Publishing (UK) Ltd.
Tel: +44 1903 204 455
Email: enquiries@avabooks.co.uk

ISBN 2-940373-54-X and 978-2-940373-54-3

10 9 8 7 6 5 4 3 2 1

Design by Gavin Ambrose
www.gavinambrose.co.uk

Production and separations by AVA Book Production
Pte. Ltd., Singapore
Tel: +65 6334 8173
Fax: +65 6259 9830
Email: production@avabooks.com.sg

The Visual Dictionary of Architecture

How to get the most out of this book 4

This book is an easy-to-use reference to the key terms used in architecture. Each entry comprises a brief textual definition along with an illustration or visual example of the point under discussion. Supplementary contextual information is also included.

Key areas addressed in this book are those terms commonly used in reference to buildings, structural designs and architectural movements.

Entries are presented in alphabetical order to provide an easy reference system.

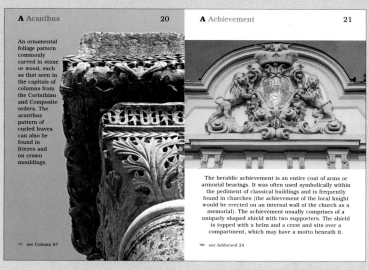

An ornamental foliage pattern commonly carved in stone or wood, such as that seen in the capitals of columns from the Corinthian and Composite orders. The acanthus pattern of curled leaves can also be found in friezes and on crown mouldings.

☞ see Column 87

The heraldic achievement is an entire coat of arms or armorial bearings. It was often used symbolically within the pediment of classical buildings and is frequently found in churches (the achievement of the local knight would be erected on an internal wall of the church as a memorial). The achievement usually comprises of a uniquely shaped shield with two supporters. The shield is topped with a helm and a crest and sits over a compartment, which may have a motto beneath it.

☞ see Addorsed 24

Each page contains a single entry and, where appropriate, a printer's hand symbol ☞ provides page references to other related and relevant entries.

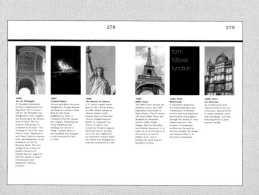

A timeline of key architectural movements, buildings and influences helps to provide historical context for selected key moments in the discipline's development.

Welcome to *The Visual Dictionary of Architecture*, a book that provides textual definitions and visual explanations for common terms found in the key areas of architecture and architectural design, and pertinent entries from the wider world of the creative arts.

This volume aims to provide a clear understanding of the many terms that are often misused or confused, such as the *Composite*, *Corinthian*, *Doric*, *Ionic* and *Tuscan* classical orders, or the difference between *Modernism* and *Classicism* or *Constructivism* and *Deconstructivism*. As you might expect, *The Visual Dictionary of Architecture* provides visual explanations in the form of illustrations and diagrams as well as photographic examples of architectural styles to illustrate each term and concept. Each visual explanation is further supported by a textual definition.

Bruce Amos

Oleg Seleznev

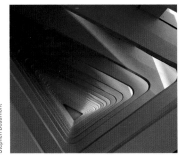

Dainis Derics

Stephen Beaumont

Architecture communicates through a range of visual devices and this book includes illustrated explanations of building's meaning and its design message, from a discussion of the process of urban design to the minutiae of the detailed design.

A clear understanding of the key terms used in architecture will help you to better understand, analyse and interpret the built world around you, articulate and formalise your ideas and ensure that you can accurately transfer those ideas to others.

Pictured (top left) is the Rococo style Great Hall of the Catherine Palace, the summer residence of the Russian tsars at Tsarskoye Selo near St. Petersburg, Russia. Also shown (top right) is the interior of the Milwaukee Art Museum.

Pictured on the facing page (left to right) is the Arch of Santa Catalina in Antigua, Guatemala, and the Church of Spilled Blood (1904) in St. Petersburg, Russia.

Pictured (right) is the Panthéon, in Paris, and (far right) is the interior of the Palais des Congrès in Montreal, which incorporates stained glass to provide light and transparency.

Also shown (facing page) is Lake Point Tower in Chicago, USA. It was designed by John Heinrich and George Schipporeit.

Architecture is a discipline that continues to evolve. The architectural timeline (page 274) shows how changes in technology and artistic style and attitude have dramatically affected how architects and designers have shaped the built environment in which we live, and how they continue to embrace advances in materials and design technology to push creative and practical boundaries. Coupled with these are the ever-changing tastes and preferences of society, which give rise to numerous schools of thought about how buildings should look and function. For example, in the twentieth century, the rise of Modernist architecture embraced technological advances, incorporating glass, steel and reinforced concrete and adopting cleaner, less adorned forms. In time, this too changed and advances in CAD (computer aided design) technology have seen the development of outrageously shaped buildings, fractals and movable architecture.

This detail of a lintel (left) with dentils and column can be found on St Ignatius Church in San Francisco, USA. Shown below is I.M. Pei's metal and glass pyramid in the courtyard of the Musée du Louvre in Paris, France.

Nina Kaiser

Florin Cirstoc

Kurt De Bruyn

Above (left) is 'Coming About', a nautically themed sculpture by Jennifer Madden situated at the entrance to Main Street in Tiburon, California, USA. The sculpture represents a series of shark fins which is a reference to the English translation of the Spanish term *tiburon* (meaning shark). Shown above (right) are medieval waterfront houses in Bruges, Belgium. The belfry tower can clearly be seen in the background.

Architects draw inspiration from innumerable sources, such as their urban environment, or by cross-referencing elements of contemporary life with those of bygone days, and delving back into the rich tradition of the arts as a means of visual stimulation. Inspiration is key to the generation of exciting architectural ideas. It is with this in mind that we hope that this book will also serve as a source of ideas to inspire your creativity.

Contents

The Dictionary

The flat slab or set found above the capital of a column. It provides a large supporting surface that receives the weight of an arch or architrave. The shape, size and decoration of an abacus can vary according to the style of architecture. The Doric order will use a thick square slab; Tuscan and Ionic, a square slab with a moulded lower edge; and Corinthian and Composite, a square slab with concave sides and the corners cut off.

☞ see Architecture 44, Architrave 45, Column 87

Can Balcioglu

The construction that supports the end of a bridge. Pictured is the Golden Gate Bridge in San Francisco, USA, which was designed by Joseph B. Strauss and completed in 1937. On the right-hand side of the image, the abutment can be seen supporting the end of the bridge. The term can also describe the masonry support that is positioned within a wall to counteract the lateral thrust of an arch.

☞ see Arch 41

An ornamental foliage pattern commonly carved in stone or wood, such as that seen in the capitals of columns from the Corinthian and Composite orders. The acanthus pattern of curled leaves can also be found in friezes and on crown mouldings.

see Column 87

The heraldic achievement is an entire coat of arms or armorial bearings. It was often used symbolically within the pediment of classical buildings and is frequently found in churches (the achievement of the local knight would be erected on an internal wall of the church as a memorial). The achievement usually comprises of a uniquely shaped shield with two supporters. The shield is topped with a helm and a crest and sits over a compartment, which may have a motto beneath it.

☞ see Addorsed 24

A defensive structure or citadel built on elevated ground close to the edge of a settlement. Acropolis derives from the Greek words *acron* (meaning 'edge'), and *polis* (meaning 'city'). They can be found throughout Europe from Bratislava in Slovakia to Edinburgh in Scotland. The most famous example is the Acropolis in Athens, Greece, which contains the Parthenon.

Pictured (left) is the Acropolis of the Old City of Jerusalem, which is situated next to the river bed, and the acropolis of Edinburgh Castle (right) in Scotland.

🕮 see Architecture 44

Scottish-born architect, Robert Adam (1728–1792) dominated the architecture of the late eighteenth century. He was a master of invention and adaptation and had an eye for ornamentation. His work is somewhere between a picturesque version of the neo-classical and a classical version of the gothic. He was equally well known as a designer of decorative interiors. Adam's great houses include Kedleston Hall in Derbyshire and Harewood House near Leeds.

Kedleston Hall (pictured left) in Derbyshire was commissioned by Sir Nathaniel Curzon in 1759. Curzon put Robert Adam in charge of the new mansion's construction after seeing Adam's garden temples in the park around the estate. Adam also co-designed Harewood House (pictured above) in West Yorkshire (1759–1771) with John Carr.

☞ see Gothic 137, Neoclassical 181

Gary Unwin

The symmetrical placement of two figures or elements back to back. Addorsed elements are commonly seen in heraldic decorations; they are often found on capitals and via the positioning of decorative sculptures and statues (such as these pictured at each end of the balustrade). The four lions guarding the base of Nelson's Column in London can be described as forming addorsed pairs. Addorsed is the opposite of affronted.

☞ see Affronted 28

Elena Ray

A natural building material made from sand, clay and organic
items such as straw. Adobe can be shaped into bricks. It is not
fired, but instead it is dried in the sun and can be used to produce
extremely hard and durable structures. It is used extensively in
hot, dry climates due to the lack of other available building
materials and has the ability to store and release heat slowly, thus
allowing buildings to remain cool during the day. Adobe is a
common building material in many parts of the world including
the Middle East and South America.

☞ see Climate 84

A border or surround that is used to frame and highlight
building elements such as doors, windows or other
openings. Traditionally an aedicule described the
columns and pediment framing a shrine in a temple.
Nowadays, the term is used to describe a wider range
of framing techniques such as the red-painted
stonework pictured above.

☞ see Architrave 45, Column 87

Dwight Smith

An anti-Victorian reaction that gathered pace towards the end of the nineteenth century and appreciated 'art for art's sake'. Followers of aestheticism (or the aesthetic movement), believed that art should be a thing of beauty rather than serving a moral or useful function. The aesthetic movement in architecture and interior design is characterised by the incorporation of natural ornamentation, such as peacock feathers (as illustrated in these decorative tiles with a peacock-based design), worked and decorative wood and a Japanese influence.

see Victorian Architecture 261

The symmetrical placement of two figures or elements so that they face one another. Affronted elements are commonly seen in architecture when they appear in heraldic decorations, such as the lion and unicorn figures seen here in the British Royal Coat of Arms on this pediment tympanum. Affronted is the opposite of addorsed.

☞ see Addorsed 24

Matt Trommer

Jennifer Stone

Any of the Spanish fortresses or castles built by the Moors during their occupation of the country. Deriving from the Arabic word *al qasr* (meaning palace or fortress), the alcazars exhibit Moorish qualities in their craftsmanship and decoration, such as the minaret-style turrets of the Alcazar of Segovia in Madrid (illustrated here). The most fabulous example of Moorish architecture is the Alhambra, in Granada, Spain.

☞ see Moorish Architecture 176

A recess or niche within the wall of a room. An alcove is often a secluded area such as a breakfast nook, and may be concealed by curtains or a balustrade. Alcove derives from the Arabic word *al quobbah*, which means 'the vault'. The term also refers to recessed features such as the aedicule pictured below.

Artur Bogacki

Areas and services within or connected to a building that add both tangible and intangible benefits to the property. In architecture, an amenity space will typically include the service areas such as toilets, heating and air ducts, lifts, escalators, parking garages, and pleasurable spaces such as gyms and swimming pools.

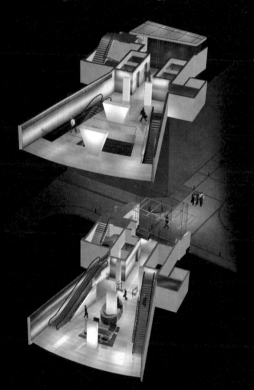

Pictured is the remodelled entrance of One Knightsbridge Green, London, designed by John Robertson Architects. The CAD drawing shows the intended position of new escalators, which have been placed within the existing core of the building.

☞ see CAD 69

A natural or man-made elliptical or oval open space, which is surrounded by seating or rising ground in which people can either sit or stand. The central area was used for public entertainment. It is a particular feature of Roman architecture, and the most famous example of an amphitheatre is the Colosseum in Rome, Italy. The precise acoustic qualities of the space allowed the audience, even those on the upper tiers of the seating, to adequately hear the entertainers.

Pictured (right) is a detail of the ruins of a Roman amphitheatre in Turkey, and (left) the El Jem Roman Colosseum in Tunisia.

☞ see Roman Architecture 219

This term collectively describes the structures, including monuments and temples, built in Egypt's Nile valley by the region's ancient civilisation from 3300BC until the country's conquest by Alexander the Great in 332BC. Ancient Egyptian architecture is characterised by use of stone, mud and brick, and a distinct lack of wood. Ancient Egyptian architecture heavily influenced the ornamentation of buildings in medieval and renaissance Europe.

Of the numerous temples and monuments remaining, the best known examples of ancient Egyptian architecture include Karnak (top left), the Great Sphinx (top right), the Great Pyramid of Giza (bottom right) and the Temple of Luxor (bottom left).

☞ see Renaissance 216

Shawn Kashou

Tadao Ando was born in Osaka, Japan in 1941. He has a reputation for sensitive and interpretive architecture with special attention to light and ambience. Ando relies on simple geometric forms to develop subtle and clear buildings with clean and atmospheric interiors. His interiors, with their clean and sparse walls, are intended as a retreat from the chaos and mayhem of modern life.

The Modern Art Museum of Fort Worth (pictured above) is constructed as a row of five rectangular blocks. They are quite low and the dominant horizontality connects with the character of the landscape. The cantilevered cast concrete roof is supported by large Y-shaped columns, which appear as human arms reaching upwards. The building is typical of Ando's sensitive and contextual approach.

☞ see Cantilever 72

The twelfth-century temple complex in Angkor,
Cambodia is an excellent example of classical Khmer
architecture. Angkor Wat is of such significance to the
people of Cambodia that it appears on the national flag
and is the country's most visited tourist attraction.
Angkor Wat is the largest and best-preserved temple in
the complex. Three rectangular galleries are contained
within its vast moat and outer wall. In the centre stands
a series of five towers. The temple is also noted for its
beautifully carved *devatas* (or deities) and bas-reliefs,
which adorn the walls.

see Bas-relief 59

An apartment (or flat) is a self-contained housing unit within a building of many units. Different apartment styles illustrate the diversity of this type of domestic architecture. Such styles include:

Apartment building: a building, tower or edifice containing many apartments.

Studio apartment: a single-roomed apartment containing a small kitchenette and a lounge/sleeping area. Also called a bedsit.

Condominium: a form of shared ownership of an individual apartment and a percentage ownership of the building's common areas.

Duplex: a two-unit apartment building or condominium that looks much like a standard house from the outside.

Shotgun or railroad flat: a narrow apartment with no hallway or corridors, with rooms built enfilade.

Garden apartment: a two-storey, semi-detached building with each floor forming a separate apartment.

Maisonette: an apartment laid out on two levels with internal stairs and its own street entrance.

Penthouse: a top-floor apartment of a multi-storey building, commanding the best views and usually finished to a very high standard.

Plattenbau: a communist-era tower block built from prefabricated concrete slabs.

Loft or warehouse conversion: a large, open apartment on a single floor, typically built in a former industrial building or warehouse.

Garage-apartment: an apartment situated above a garage.

Granny flat: a small, self-contained apartment built at the back of, or as an addition to an upper or lower level, of the main house.

A hole or opening. In architecture, an aperture would typically be a window or door, and it is used both as a decorative or practical feature. It can facilitate visual or physical movement or act as a means of allowing light to pass through a wall. An example is the oculus in the roof of the Panthéon in Rome, Italy.

Pictured is the National Bank of Slovakia by Martin Kusy and Pavol Panak. The aperture in the concrete platform provides views of the tower above (shown left) and details of the tiny decorative holes that feature in its wall (shown right).

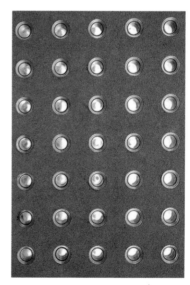

Jozef Sedmak

☞ see Panthéon 193

The act of taking something and applying it to a different situation. Pictured below is a house that is styled like an igloo, complete with a dome and arched entrance. The architect has appropriated the character of an igloo's particular building style and reused it in a manner that utilises very different materials, in a different climate and place, and with a different purpose, thus making a postmodern statement about what a house should look like.

☞ see Arch 41, Domes 98, House Styles 141, Postmodernism 207

The Islamic artistic patterns and aesthetic styles
that commonly adorn the buildings of Arabic-influenced
architecture, such as those that decorate the ceiling
of this mosque (pictured). Arabesque decoration is
often intricate and whimsical, with geometric patterns
overlaid with flowing lines, completely covering the
surface with spirals and zig-zags. The human figure
is never used. The Alhambra in Granada, Spain,
contains many features that display the repeated
arabesque geometric patterns.

An enclosed passage or walkway that is covered with a series of arches or vaults supported on columns or piers. Arcades may be used to house small shops and boutiques and are atmospheric and charming environments. Arcades are sometimes buried deep within a building, but conversely can be full height with a glazed roof, such as the Galleria Umberto in Naples, Italy (pictured). The term is often confused with 'colonnade', which in fact describes a sequence of columns open on at least one side and joined at their entablature.

see Colonnade 85

A curved structure that spans an opening and supports weight above it. An arch is capable of spanning a much larger opening than a lintel. Arches have been a common feature of architecture throughout history, ever since they were first developed in the Indus Valley (c.2500BC). Each subsequent civilisation has developed and reworked the arch to create its own distinct and identifiable style, such as those illustrated below. Arches are traditionally built from wedge-shaped stone or brick blocks that transfer the weight they support to the side supporting elements. The compression from the weight above is important to the structural integrity of the arch.

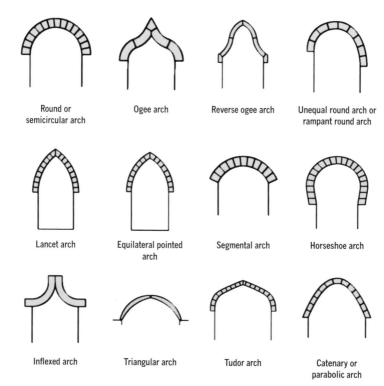

Round or
semicircular arch

Ogee arch

Reverse ogee arch

Unequal round arch or
rampant round arch

Lancet arch

Equilateral pointed
arch

Segmental arch

Horseshoe arch

Inflexed arch

Triangular arch

Tudor arch

Catenary or
parabolic arch

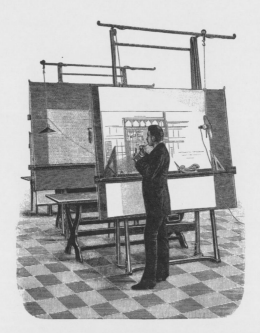

A person qualified to design and supervise the construction of buildings or other large structures. The architect will interpret the needs and requirements of the client and combine these with other issues such as site conditions, building and planning regulations and technological considerations to create the design of the building. The architect will first draw the building design in detail before overseeing its construction. Architects contribute to the shape of our built environment and, as such, have a responsibility to creatively and conscientiously inform the character and nature of experience.

Architectural styles change and adapt through time as materials, building construction technology, and theoretical and conceptual ideas evolve. This brief timeline lists key periods notable for their distinct architectural styles.

Date	Name	☞ See page
1100–146BC	Ancient Greek	–
1200–3000BC	Mesolithic	–
1300–1600BC	Gothic	137
1500–1650BC	Renaissance	216
3000–1800BC	Neolithic Age	–
1800–550BC	Bronze Age	–
550BC–AD43	Iron Age	–
AD43–400	Roman	219
400–650	Dark Age	–
650–1066	Anglo-Saxon	–
1066–1189	Norman	183
1189–1307	Early English	102
1307–1350	Decorated	95
1327–1520	Perpendicular	198
1520–1558	Tudor	255
1558–1603	Elizabethan	108
1603–1625	Jacobean	–
1625–1689	Stuart	–
1689–1714	Queen Anne (Baroque)	57
1714–1830	Georgian	133
1810–1830	Regency (Late Georgian)	213
1837–1901	Victorian	261
1901–1914	Edwardian	–
1919–1933	Bauhaus	60
1920–1939	Art Deco	47
1922–Present day	International Style (Modern)	142
1933–1955	Stalinist Empire	241
1940–Present day	Postmodernist/Deconstructivist	207/94

The discipline of designing buildings and other structures in the built environment. Architecture comes from the Greek word *arkhitekton* meaning 'master builder'. The practice of architecture combines the required function, materials and budget available, with conceptual aspects to produce the final building. Architecture is a subject that is continually evolving, due to advances in technology, expectations of the users, theoretical ideas and building regulations. Great architecture is variously defined as that which combines all the above elements in a way that strikes an emotional chord within a person.

Pictured is a page from Volume I of Ephraim Chambers' *Cyclopaedia* (1728), a universal dictionary of arts and sciences. This page features definitions of the various architectural elements concerned with the column.

The lowest of the three divisions of an entablature or beam in classical building. An architrave usually sits above a column and its capital. An architrave can also refer to the moulded frame that surrounds a door or a window.

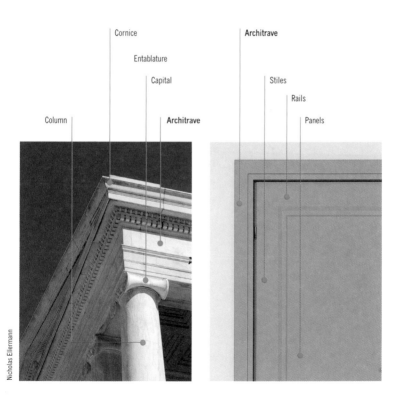

Cornice

Entablature

Capital

Column

Architrave

Architrave

Stiles

Rails

Panels

Nicholas Ellermann

☞ see **Column 87, Cornice 93, Door 99, Window 265**

architecture
+
ecology

An architectural design concept developed by architect Paolo Soleri for the construction of large structures in order to provide housing for dense populations. Arcology is the fusion of the words 'architecture' and 'ecology', and the concept promotes the efficient use of natural resources in living areas called hyperstructures. Hyperstructures are characterised by vast buildings in megacities such as those policed by Judge Dread in the *2000AD* comic. Hyperstructures have yet to capture the public imagination despite hotels and office buildings now being built on an ever-grander scale. The experimental town of Arcosanti in central Arizona, USA is an example of a city embodying the principles of arcology.

☞ see Architecture 44

A style of architecture and design prevalent during the 1920s and 1930s. Art Deco architecture was characterised by stylised natural forms, geometrical shapes and symmetrical designs. The style was influenced by other early twentieth century movements including Art Nouveau, the Bauhaus and Futurism, and was concurrent with the International Style. The name is derived from the 1925 Exposition Internationale des Arts Decoratifs et Industriels Modernes, which was held in Paris.

Pictured (left) is the Art-Deco style lobby of The Daily Express Building in London. The interior was designed by Robert Atkinson, and refurbished to its former glory by John Robertson Architects. Shown above is the Empire State Building in New York City. It was designed by Shreve, Lamb and Harmon, and built in 1931 at the height of the Art Deco period.

Franck Chazot

An architectural style that originated in the 1880s and lasted until the early twentieth century. Art Nouveau was a style that reacted to the Victorian practice of pastiche, and was deliberately modern; indeed the style is referred to as *Modernismo* in Spain. Architects such as Charles Rennie Mackintosh, Antoni Gaudi and Victor Horta practised it; they adapted sinuous natural forms and applied them to objets d'art, and to the shapes of windows, doors and mouldings. These natural or organic forms of architecture often incorporated floral and other plant-inspired motifs. Well-recognised examples of Art Nouveau architecture are the entrances to the Paris Metro, which were designed by Hector Guimard.

see Mackintosh, Charles Rennie 157

An architecture style inspired by the work of John Ruskin and Philip Webb, which evolved as a reaction to the industrialisation of the Victorian era. The Arts and Crafts Movement placed importance upon simple medieval styles and manual skills and it believed the Industrial Revolution distanced the humans from their own creativity. The main exponents of this movement included William Morris, Edwin Lutyens, Charles Francis Annesley Voysey and Frank Lloyd Wright.

Pictured is a plan for the Red House (1859) in Kent, England. Designed by Philip Webb, it is regarded as one of the greatest examples of the Arts and Crafts genre.

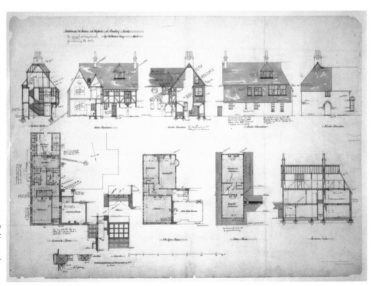

☞ see Lloyd Wright, Frank 154

WH Chow

A term used to describe a facade with no columns or pilasters. The origins of the style can be traced back to the Romans and their movement away from the column and towards the wall. The Palazzo Strozzi in Florence, Italy (pictured right), which was completed in about 1536, is a huge building with rusticated stone elevations and harmonious proportions. The Palazzo Vecchio (pictured left), or Palazzo della Signoria, was once the town hall and dates from about 200 years earlier. Its design presents a strong fortified exterior with bell towers.

Rachelle Burnside

The lack of symmetry. In architecture this could describe a building in which there are no lines of balance. Asymmetric architecture has a bias or weighting to one side or area, such as the twisting 44 metre observation tower on the MH de Young Museum in Golden Gate Park, San Francisco, California. The tower is placed to one side of the long, low, copper-clad building. Swiss architects Herzog and De Meuron collaborated with Fong and Chan to design the museum in 2005.

☞ see Symmetry 247

An atrium was once used to describe the inner courtyard of a Roman domestic building; it was open to the sky and surrounded by an overhanging roof. The term is now used to describe a large internal public space, which is usually the full height of the building and has a glazed roof. The atrium will often contain elements of circulation, such as stairs and elevators.

Pictured (left) is an internal view of the central atrium in the 33-storey Grand Hyatt hotel in Shanghai. The hotel is located between the 53rd and 87th floors of the Jin Mao Tower, which was designed in 2005 by Skidmore, Owens and Merrill. Also pictured (below) is a detail of the atrium in the Vatican Museum in Rome, Italy.

☞ see Storey 244

An imaginary line that usually runs through the centre
of a space or building, an axis is used as a planning
device and is related to symmetry. Axial planning can
be used to arrange a building or interior in straight lines
or in a way that prioritises certain qualities (such as a
view through the space) or emphasises hierarchy. This
is quite different to a centrally planned building, which
will radiate from the centre point.

The strong central axis that runs through the Alhambra in Spain is reinforced by the
channel of water at floor level.

Rafael Ramirez Lee

☞ see Symmetry 247

A handrail or coping that is supported by a series of balusters or posts, and runs horizontally along the front of a gallery or balcony. A balustrade is typically made from stone although wood or other materials can be used. Balustrades are normally an external architectural feature although they can also be used internally. They should not be confused with a banister, which is a handrail that runs up and around a staircase.

St Peter's Basilica in the Vatican (left) has a strong classical balustrade edging the patio.

This palace on the edge of a canal in Venice, Italy (pictured above) displays an ornate balustrade on its upper floor.

☞ see Banister 55

A supported handrail built on to a staircase to provide rigidity and protection. The banister is usually supported by vertical pickets or balusters. It may connect at either end to a newel post that is firmly attached to the floor joist, or a half-newel post connected to the wall. Other banister features may include a spiral volute, if the staircase ends with a bullnose step, and the handrail may have a gooseneck (a vertical section that connects it to a higher handrail on a balcony or landing).

Pictured is the refurbished staircase in The Daily Express Building in London created by John Robertson Architects. It has a smooth continuous handrail without pickets.

☞ **see Balustrade 54**

The Barcelona (or German) Pavilion was built as a temporary structure for the 1929 International Exhibition by Ludwig Mies van der Rohe. It was designed to project an image of an international, open and modern German state. The building was composed of sliding vertical and horizontal planes, which were tied together by the tight formation of eight columns. The composition was not symmetrical, but it was balanced, and this produced a sense of perpetual movement within the intense rhythm of spaces and planes.

see International Style 142, Mies van der Rohe, Ludwig 168

A European style of architecture of the seventeenth and eighteenth centuries. It was based upon the transformation of classical forms with an inventive use of space and decoration. It was characterised by ornate detail, exuberant curvaceous decoration and grand sweeping gestures with spatially complex compositions. Examples of Baroque architecture include the façade in St Peter's Basilica in Rome and the Palace of Versailles.

Pictured below is the south elevation of Chatsworth House in Derbyshire, England. Both the south and the east fronts of the building were built under the direction of William Talman and the house is considered to be a key development in the history of English Baroque architecture.

Stephen Mulcahey

☞ see Classicism 83

Marek Slusarczyk

A large, roofed Roman hall within which business and legal matters were traditionally conducted. A basilica typically has interior colonnades that divide the space lengthways, and the divisions provide aisles. The apse is typically located at the Eastern end. Following the Roman Empire's adoption of Christianity, basilicas began to be used as places of worship and became large and important churches upon which special ceremonial rights were conferred by the Pope.

Pictured above is the ornate ceiling decoration from a basilica in Rome.

☞ see Colonnade 85, Empire 109, Roman Architecture 219

Vova Pomortzeff

A method for sculpting an image into the surface of a flat piece
of stone. A bas-relief gives low contrast; the form of the image
projects only slightly from the background (which can be seen
in this detail of an apsara, which is a female spirit of the clouds
and water). This bas-relief can be found on the Bayon Temple
in the Angkor complex, Cambodia. The temple was built in the
thirteenth century by King Jayavarman VII and features
bas-reliefs that depict mythical and historic events.

see Angkor Wat 35

pictured (left) is the bauhaus building in dessau, germany, which was designed by walter gropius and his partner adolf meyer.

an art and design school that opened in 1919 under the direction of renowned architect walter gropius. the bauhaus, which translates as 'house for building', aimed to provide a fresh pedagogical approach that focused on producing designs according to first principles rather than by following historic precedent. bauhaus architecture rejected decorative detailing in favour of pure form without ornamentation. it is characterised by economic and geometrical forms such as flat roofs, smooth façades and cubic shapes with open floor plans and low-key white, grey, beige or black colouring.

the evolution of bauhaus was guided and influenced by the varying approaches of its different directors. the 1926 bauhaus building in dessau, germany typifies the approach of walter gropius and his partner, adolf meyer. the swiss communist architect hannes meyer (the second director of the school, 1928–1930) then moved the architectural focus towards functionality. ludwig mies van der rohe essentially imposed his own aesthetic vision on the school when he became director in 1930.

A vertical division of a building that is made apparent
not by walls, but by columns, buttresses or fenestration.
The term can also refer to an angular or curved element
that projects from the walls of a building, thus forming
a bay within a room.

Illustrated is the rear portal of the Reichstag in Berlin, Germany, which was
remodelled by Foster + Partners in 1999. The portal has five bays, three of
which have been glazed.

see Window 265

A very rich classical style of architecture that originated from the École des Beaux-Arts in late nineteenth century France. Beaux-Arts placed emphasis on Italian-Roman architecture and French and Italian baroque styles. Public buildings were composed in both plan and elevation, their function was expressed on the façade, and the structural hierarchy was clearly visible. The ornamentation had flamboyance and gusto with the use of coloured marble and mosaics.

Pictured is Palais Garnier (Paris Opéra) in Paris, which was completed by Charles Garnier in 1875. It is thought to be the epitome of the Beaux-Arts style.

🖝 see Baroque 57, Sculpturesque 225

Jozef Sedmak

The upper room in a tower that contains one or more
bells. The height allows for the peals of the bells to
reach over a wide distance. A belfry is typically found
as part of a church or other civic building and is often
a free-standing tower. The term, perhaps surprisingly,
has no connection with bell, but is derived from the
French word *berfrei*.

Illustrated is the *campanile* (the Italian word for belfry) of St Mark's in Venice, Italy.

Sean Elliott

A contemporary architectural movement typified by building designs that incorporate organic, bulbous, amoeba-shaped forms, which are created using CAD (computer aided design) software. Blobitecture was a derogatory term first coined by William Safire in the *New York Times Magazine* in 2002. However, the word's use has since evolved to incorporate all curved or oddly shaped buildings.

Pictured is the Sage Centre in Gateshead, England. An example of blobitecture, this musical education and performance centre was designed by Foster + Partners and opened in 2004. The building features an undulating glass and stainless steel exterior that houses three music halls. One of the music halls was built as an acoustically perfect space; its ceiling panels may be raised and lowered to change the sound profile of the room.

see CAD 69

The bricks in a wall, house or other structure in terms of their type or layout. A stretcher is the long edge of a brick, while a header is the short end. The bond is the method of laying the bricks to give strength, stability and decoration.

Diaper
This pattern features a repetitive surface decoration that is achieved through the use of different coloured bricks. The difference in colour decoration was traditionally achieved by incorporating of flared headers (bricks that had been oven-fired).

Quarter stretcher bond
A common brickwork pattern that uses whole bricks, which are quick to lay. Bricks are laid so that they overlap one another by a quarter.

Header bond
A pattern made using the header face of the brick. The colour of this pattern is influenced by the use of a large amount of mortar.

English bond
Alternating courses of headers and stretchers to produce a quarter bond look.

English garden wall bond
Similar to English bond, but with the header course at every third, fifth or seventh stretcher course.

Flemish bond
Alternating headers and stretchers in the same course, with headers placed centrally over the stretchers.

Flemish garden wall bond
Flemish bond variant with one header placed at every third stretcher. Also called Sussex bond.

An architectural style that emerged in 1954 and was popular until the 1970s. Its distinguishing feature was the use of naked concrete. Brutalism derives from the French phrase *béton brut* meaning 'raw concrete', a term first used by French (Swiss-born) architect Le Corbusier. Brutalist architecture features big, repetitive, angular geometries, with textured board-marked surfaces.

Illustrated is the National Theatre (1965–76) on London's South Bank, which was designed by Denys Lasden. Clearly visible are the strong interlocking geometric forms, which are constructed from rough concrete.

David Burrows

☞ see Reinforced Concrete 214

A structure built against (or projecting from) a wall in order to provide additional support. The development of the buttress allowed masonry buildings to reach new heights by providing a mechanism for supporting the weight of high walls. Buttresses and flying buttresses are key features of Gothic churches.

Buttress
The additional support structure built against a wall.

Flying buttress
A half-arch structure in which the elevated end provides additional support to the main load-bearing wall.

Diagonal buttress
A support built from the junction or corner of the wall, it forms a 135-degree angle between the buttress and each wall.

see Gothic 137

Bora Ucak

The architecture of the Early Christian, Greek-speaking eastern Roman Empire from 330AD until the fall of Constantinople in 1453. Byzantine architecture characteristically features the domed arch, the use of a centrally planned, cross-in-square ground plan, and interiors that are typically decorated with painted and mosaic biblical scenes. Byzantine architecture heavily influenced the later Ottoman architecture, which is characterised by generous inner spaces housed in large domes.

Pictured are an illustration of the Fountain of Sultan Ahmed in Istanbul, Turkey (top); the Hagia Sophia or the Holy Wisdom Temple in Istanbul, Turkey (middle); and the inner dome of the Selimiye Mosque in Edirne, Turkey built by Mimar Sinan (1568–1574) for Sultan Selim II (right).

see Arch 41, Dome 98

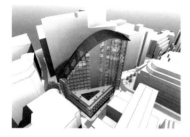 

A suite of computer-based drafting tools used by architects and engineers to design buildings. Computer-aided design (CAD) allows architects and designers to produce detailed three-dimensional or two-dimensional drawings of buildings and their component parts. Computer-aided design and modelling has opened the door for architects to use construction materials more creatively. It has also allowed the development of postmodernist designs and genres such as blobitecture. CAD is continually evolving, and provides, amongst many other things: the generation of engineering drawings from solid models; the ability to validate designs against specifications and design rules; the ability to simulate designs without prototype building; and the ability to output design data direct to manufacturing facilities, as well many other things.

Pictured is a typical example of a CAD drawing by John Robertson Architects.

Santiago Calatrava was born in 1951 in Spain and trained as both a structural engineer and an architect. His designs are influenced by nature and natural forms – in fact many of his bridges are almost organic: they appear quite animal-like and seem to have a natural tension. Long structural members stretch and arch to bridge large gaps as if they were bones with sinuous tissue attached.

Shown here is Calatrava's City of Arts and Sciences building in Valencia, Spain. It was an extremely ambitious project intended to fill the dry riverbed with public facilities and thus link the city centre with the sea. To enforce this relationship, Calatrava's design is a series of sculptural buildings that are tied together with pools of running water.

David Corral

Gary Calder

A covering erected to provide protection from the elements or to emphasise a particular activity. A canopy comprises a cover or hood that is made of metal or fabric and elevated and supported by a framework. A canopy can provide emphasis, offer protection or accentuate an architectural element.

A fabric canopy offering protection from the elements (above), and a metal and glass canopy that emphasises the building's entrance (right).

Wendy Kaveney Photography

A structure in which a beam appears to be unsupported at one end. The beam (A), projects further than its supporting column (B). The load pressing down on the supported end of the beam (C) counteracts the toppling motion pushing at D; this allows for the construction of overhanging structures that do not require bracing.

Cantilevers are used widely in bridge and balcony design, as typified by the railway bridge over the Firth of Forth (shown above). This conceptual sketch by John Robertson Architects (pictured below) shows how the proposed building is cantilevered from the first floor.

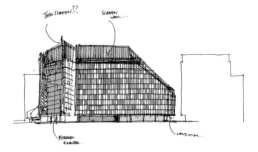

Cape Cod
A seventeenth-century building style originating from New England, USA. Cape Cod houses are typically 1.5 storeys high and feature a low, broad frame with a steep, pitched roof, gables and a central chimney. They are also characterised by wooden weather boarding or shingle exteriors with shutters.

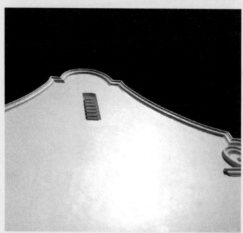

Cape Dutch
An architectural style originating from the houses built by Dutch settlers in the Western Cape of South Africa. These houses feature round shaped gables and are normally built in an H-shape with wings that flank the front section.

☞ see Section Drawing 228

This engraving of the Piazza del Campidoglio in Rome (above) by Etienne Dupérac features Michelangelo's oval-shaped patio.

This replica statue of equestrian Marcus Aurelius (below), can be found at the Capitoline Hill.

The highest and most sacred of the seven hills of Rome, and home to the Piazza del Campidoglio (1536–1546), which was designed and created by Renaissance artist and architect Michelangelo Buonarroti. Michelangelo harnessed the sloping, trapezoid space by surrounding it with three palaces, which could be accessed via the Cordonata Staircase. Michelangelo's design reversed the classical orientation of the Capitoline, turning Rome's civic centre to face away from the Roman forum and towards St Peter's Basilica, a move that echoed the politics of the time.

Girard Cheron

A form of working materials such as wood, stone
or rock to produce either three-dimensional objects
or bas-relief designs.

Pictured are bas-relief letters carved into the wooden door of Antoni Gaudi's Sagrada
Familia Cathedral in Barcelona, Spain.

☞ see Bas-relief 59, Gaudí, Antonio 128

Arrow slits
Narrow openings in castle walls through which archers could shoot. Also called 'arrow loops' or meurtriéres, they differ in width, length and shape and design. Some slits took the form of a cross and some incorporated an oilette – a round base opening that gives an archer a wider field of view.

Bailey
An enclosed courtyard overlooked by the motte (or keep) of a motte-and-bailey castle, which were built in the eleventh and twelfth centuries in France and England following the Norman Conquest.

Barbican
An outer defence element of a castle. Often a heavily fortified tower above a gate or drawbridge of a castle. Barbicans were connected to city walls via a walled road referred to as 'the neck'.

Batter
The sloped outside base of the curtain wall used to bounce rocks on to attacking forces.

Battlement
Crenellated defensive top edge of a wall that provides a defender with protection, but its periodic cut-out portions allow the discharge of weapons. The solid widths between crenels are called merlons.

Drawbridge
A wooden bridge, capable of being raised or lowered and used as a passageway or gate.

Embrasure
An opening in a wall through which arrows or bolts may be fired.

Enceinte
The fortified enclosure of the castle precincts, usually outlined by a defensive wall surmounted by a parapet or walkway from which the castle can be defended.

Keep
The commanding tower and residential structure of a castle functioning as the last line of defence.

Machicolation holes
Holes in the battlement floor that allowed defenders to shoot directly below as well as drop stones and pour boiling oil on attackers. Similar holes in the ceilings of the gatehouse are called 'murder holes'.

Portcullis
A grille or gate made of wood or metal that forms part of the fortified entrance to many medieval castles. From the French porte coleice, meaning 'sliding gate', a portcullis was an important line of defence during an attack, and could be raised or lowered quickly via chains or ropes.

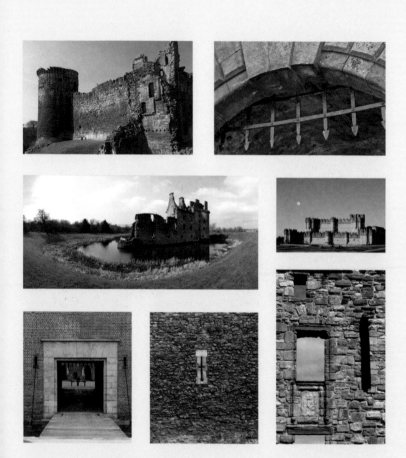

Pictured (clockwise from top left) are: the ruined battlements and tower of a castle; a portcullis gate in raised position; the fortress of Castillo de Coca in Segovia, Spain; an arrow slit in St Andrew's Castle in Fife, Scotland; an arrow slit on a defensive wall at the Tower of London; and a drawbridge and raised portcullis at Fort Pulaski, Georgia, USA; and Caerlaverock Castle, in Dumfriesshire, Scotland.

Large and often ornately decorated building used by the Christian faith for religious worship. A cathedral is a bishop's seat and the central church of a diocese. Cathedrals can be found in most main European cities.

Cologne Cathedral

This is the second-tallest gothic structure in the world, and it took over 600 years to complete (between 1248–1880). Cologne Cathedral has two 157-metre towers and the largest church façade in the world, making it one of Germany's most famous landmarks. Built to house the relics of the Magi, the majority of its construction occurred in the nineteenth century following the surviving medieval plans and drawings.

The Cathedral of Christ the Saviour

This is the tallest and largest Eastern Orthodox Church in the world, and is located on the bank of the Moskva River in Moscow, Russia. The Cathedral was completed in 1860 and features elaborate frescoes. Following the death of Lenin, the cathedral was dynamited in 1931 to make way for the never-completed Palace of Soviets. Following the end of Communist rule, the church was rebuilt and consecrated in 2000.

☞ see Gothic 137

Pictured are the side aisle of Århus Cathedral in Århus, Denmark (top); and an ornate floral boss (below).

Aisle
A lateral division that is parallel to, and divided by pillars from, a nave, choir or transept.

Ambulatory
A circular aisle that wraps around the apse.

Apse
The semicircular or polygonal termination to the choir or aisles of a church.

Aumbry (or ambry)
A cupboard or recess within a sanctuary or chapel wall that often contains the church's sacred vessels and chalices.

Boss
The highly decorated carvings found in ceilings and used to conceal breaks in the vault work.

Buttress
A mass of stone built to add additional support to a wall of great height.

Chancel
Part of the altar for the clergy or choir, bordered by railings.

Chapels (or chantries)
Recesses on the sides of aisles in cathedrals and abbey churches.

Cinquefoil
An ornamental design of five pendants in a circular ring surrounding a window or panel.

Clerestory
The upper storey of a church that rises above the aisle roof; it is often lined with a series of windows, which allow extra light into the interior.

Cloister
A covered arcade or walkway that usually runs around the sides of a quadrangle.

Crocket
A small ornament (typically depicting stylised foliage) projecting from the sloping angles of pinnacles or spires.

Dripstone
A small stone incorporated into door or window jambs to direct rain water clear of the opening.

Finial
The top or finishing stone of a pinnacle.

Flying buttress
A buttress that is arched at the top and engages with a main wall to give additional support. Flying butresses are a common feature of Gothic architecture.

Gargoyle
A spout carved in the shape of an animal or demon, which drains rain water from the roof of a building.

Green man
A decorative Gothic carving characterised by a human face sprouting from foliage.

Nave
The main internal area of a church or cathedral that is used by the congregation. The word comes from the Latin term navis, meaning 'a ship'.

Reredos
A decorative screen behind the altar, usually highly carved.

Pictured are cloisters in a church in Madrid, Spain (top); and a green man water feature in Aix-en-Provence, France (below).

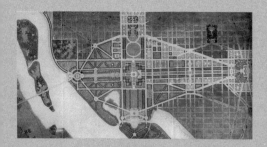

A progressive reform movement that flourished during 1890–1900 in North America, and sought to use town planning as a means to overcome the problems of city life. The City Beautiful Movement endeavoured to create attractive urban environments and generate a feeling of well-being with the development of harmonious public spaces and monumental architecture. The movement borrowed from the Beaux-Arts aesthetic, and its architecture is characterised by colonnaded domes for public buildings. The movement's influence is particularly evident in the cities of Chicago, Detroit and Washington DC.

Top left: The McMillan Plan (1901) for the development of Washington DC, USA, which was formulated by the Senate Park Improvement Commission.

Top right: The National Mall in Washington DC, USA, an area of gardens and ponds created as part of the McMillan Plan, extending from the grounds of the Washington Monument to the US Capitol building.

Above: The cupola of the Colorado State Capitol Building in Denver, Colorado, which was designed by Elijah Myers at the beginning of the twentieth century.

☞ see Beaux-Arts 62, Colonnade 85, Monumentalism 175

The external covering or skin of material over a structure. It may be used for environmental or decorative purposes.

Pictured (left) is 120 Fleet Street, in London, a project undertaken by John Robertson Architects. The new building's frontage is both glass and stone-clad. Time-lapse photography (above) shows the erection of the structure, and how the addition of cladding brings the final form to life.

Xavier Marchant

A return to the principles of Greek and Roman art and architecture. There have been a number of classical revivals, but the most well known is the neoclassical movement that began in the mid-eighteenth century.

Bartłomiej Kwieciszewski

Shown above is L'église de la Madeleine, in Paris, France. It was designed as a temple to the glory of Napoleon's army. Pictured left is Lazienki Palace in Warsaw, Poland. It features an entablature carried by Corinthian order pilasters and crowned by a balustrade that bears statues of mythological figures.

☞ see Neoclassical 181, Orders 187, Roman Architecture 219

Helmut Watson

Khafizow Harisowich

The temperature and precipitation profile of a location. Climate is one of the most fundamental concerns of architecture because one of the primary functions of a building is to provide protection and shelter from the elements. This consideration informs the choice of materials to be used in a structure's design. Architecture traditionally responds to the challenges of a site's climate through the use of locally available materials. For example, ice is used to build igloos in the harsh Arctic environment while terracotta tiles and adobe walls are often found in the architecture of southern Spain to help withstand heat and rainfall.

Pictured (above left) is the entrance hall to The Ice Hotel in Quebec, Canada, an extraordinary concept that is necessarily rebuilt every year. Shown right is a detail from the roof of a building in Crimea, Ukraine. Its pan-tiles allow vast amounts of water to quickly drain away.

see Materials 161

Andrea Ferguson

A row of columns joined by an entablature or by arches.
A colonnade may be straight or curved and can be used
in a number of different ways. The name given to a
colonnade will depend upon its situation. For instance,
when positioned in front of a building it is called a
portico; if it comprises single columns it is a screen;
if it encloses an open court it is a peristyle; and if it
encloses the passage around a courtyard it is a cloister.
A colonnade is unlike an arcade as it does not house
or create any discrete spaces or rooms.

see Arcade 40, Arch 41, Column 87

Emma Pullicino

The Colosseum in Rome is perhaps one of the most famous examples of Roman architecture. It was initiated in AD70 by Vespian and completed ten years later by emperor Titus. Covering six acres, the Colosseum is by far the largest Roman amphitheatre, and is a free-standing 48-metre-high, 189-metre-long and 156-metre-wide structure with a three-storey monumental façade consisting of arcades framed by decorative Tuscan, Ionic, and Corinthian semi-columns. Above these, there would originally have been another level of timber seating. Below the stage was a complex arrangements of passageways, cages, lifts and ramps used by the performers and animals.

☞ see Façade 113, Orders 187

David Pedre

Whether one of the Doric, Tuscan, Ionic, Corinthian or Composite orders, a column is a vertical element that allows the weight of a structure to pass through compression to structural elements below it. A column consists of the base, shaft and capital, and is commonly found supporting arches, beams or entablature.

Columns typically have a larger diameter at the bottom than the top, which makes them appear straighter and taller. Most have a convex shape called entasis, which compensates for the concave illusion produced when the sides are perfectly straight.

Pictured is part of the remains of the Temple of Olympian Zeus in Athens, Greece (completed in AD2). It was the largest temple in Greece during the Hellenistic and Roman periods.

see Entasis 110, Orders 187, Roman Architecture 219

The Composite column is a late Roman combination of elements from the Ionic and Corinthian orders. Proportionally it is the same as the Corinthian, and includes the volutes of the Ionic order and the foliated capitals of the Corinthian. Composite columns can also feature decorative echinus – the bit above the volute but below the abacus – and plant designs with egg-and-dart ornamentation.

Ionic + Corinthian

Robert Beyers

☞ see Abacus 18, Corinthian 92, Ionic 143, Orders 187, Volute 264

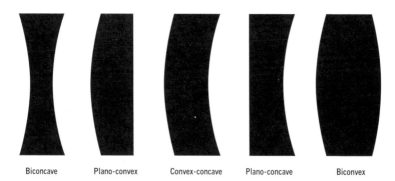

| Biconcave | Plano-convex | Convex-concave | Plano-concave | Biconvex |

An outline that curves or bulges inwards (concave) or outwards (convex). As material and construction technology continues to advance, architects have obtained greater freedom to create buildings and can thus move away from the cuboid structures of modernism by introducing more curved surfaces.

The 365-metre diameter O2 building (formerly the Millennium Dome) in London, was created by architect Richard Rogers and is the largest single-roofed structure in the world (right). It has twelve 100-metre-high support towers and a plano-convex shape. In contrast, the building overlooking the Maas River in the Netherlands (left) has a distinctly concave shape.

Marco Regalia

☞ see Alcove 30, Dome 98

A roughly drawn sketch that outlines the visual concept
and appearance of a building. A conceptual sketch may
take the form of a moment of inspiration noted down as
quickly as possible, or a more studied outline of how a
proposed building or scheme will look.

Pictured is a conceptual sketch by John Robertson Architects for the
Warner Stand at Lord's Cricket Ground in London.

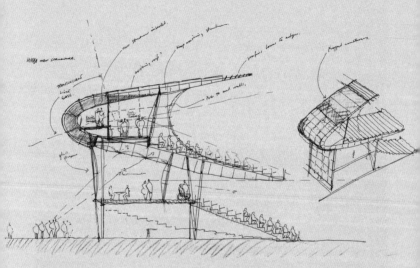

Constructivism continues to bear influence as architects explore increasingly dynamic and abstract shapes. This can be seen in buildings such as Frank Gehry's Vitra Design Museum, in Weil am Rhein, Germany (pictured below).

A movement that originated in early twentieth-century Communist Russia. Constructivism celebrated movement, industry and modern materials, and sought to break with the past through a combination of utopian ideals and abstract architectonic form. Constructivism employed three-dimensional abstraction to create futuristic buildings such as Yakov Chernikhov's Hammer and Sickle Architectural Fantasy (pictured above).

A Greek and Roman classical order. The Corinthian order is identified by its slender fluted column and an ornate capital decorated with acanthus leaves and scrolls. This order was little used in Greek architecture but became popular during Roman times. Corinthian column flutes may be filleted with rods nestling within. Beading or chains of husks may also be included as it offers more opportunities for variation than the other orders.

Pictured is a detail of a Corinthian column and its distinctive carved capital. Notice how the abacus above the capital has a rosette in its centre and concave sides to match the capital's scrolling corners.

☞ **see Column 87**

Michael Smith

A projecting horizontal decorative moulding that crowns a building. The cornice is the top projecting section of the entablature. The word originates from the Italian word *cornicone*, meaning 'ledge'.

Any element that projects slightly at the top of the building, and therefore helps throw the rain away from the walls, can be described as a cornice. The top sloping elements of a portico are also described as a cornice.

Pictured is a detail of the cornice at the United States Custom House in Charleston, South Carolina, which was built between 1853–1879.

A branch of postmodern architecture and theory that
developed during the late 1980s and is characterised
by ideas of fragmentation and non-linear design
processes. It rejects such maxims as 'form follows
function', preferring to distort and give an appearance
of controlled chaos.

This style is clearly illustrated by the design of the Guggenheim Museum in Bilbao, Spain. It
was created by Canadian-born architect Frank Gehry and features radically sculpted, organic
contours. It has been one of the most widely recognised deconstructivist buildings since its
opening in 1997.

see Gehry, Frank 130

Philip Lange

Early English Period (c.1180–1275)
Decorated Period (c.1275–1380)
Perpendicular Period (c.1380–1520)

A style of English architecture that developed in the thirteenth century and would evolve into the later Perpendicular style. Architecture of this period is characterised by its window openwork that features parallel mullions which cross and intersect to create a stone matrix of tracery that fills the top part of the window. Tracery style changed from being geometrical to a flowing curvilinear style at the start of the period.

Pictured is the decorated western elevation of Wells Cathedral, in Somerset. It is England's largest medieval church and is a fine example of the elaborate window tracery typical of the period.

A small square-shaped block that forms a repeat decorative pattern in a cornice. A dentil typically projects as far as it is wide, with a spacing interval of half its width.

Pictured is a neoclassical European building that features a sequence of dentils within an entablature above a series of Corinthian columns.

☞ see Column 87, Corinthian 92, Cornice 93

A Dutch artistic movement founded in 1917 that sought to express the utopian ideal of spiritual harmony and order. De Stijl (or the style), focused on pure abstraction and universality through a reduction to the essentials of form and colour. They advocated the use of clean untextured planes decorated with pure dense primary colours. Mies van der Rohe was a leading proponent of the De Stijl movement, although it was the Dutch designer and architect Gerrit Thomas Rietveld (1888–1964) who designed the Schröder House (1923), the only building created in accordance with De Stijl design principles.

Pictured (clockwise from the left) is a page from the November 1921 issue of *De Stijl* magazine; 'Arithmetische Compositie' (1924) created by Theo van Doesburg; and the Schröder House, which was designed by Gerrit Thomas Rietveld.

☞ see Mies van der Rohe, Ludwig 168

Pictured are the black domes of the Russian church in Tallinn, Estonia (top); a detail of the domes of St Basil's Cathedral in Moscow, Russia (below left); and the Dome of the Rock on Temple Mount in Jerusalem, Israel (below right).

Veronika Trofer

Dmitry Bodrov

Pavel Bernshtam

A concave structural element erected upon a circular base, and usually the shape of a semi-sphere. A dome has a curved surface and functions much like an arch, but provides support in all directions. Larger domes often have two or even three layers: the top and bottom are decorative, while the centre layer is structural and supports the other two. Domes can be segmental, semicircular, pointed or bulbous.

see Arch 41

A swinging or sliding plane usually made from wood or metal, which is used for closing an opening in a wall. A door can cover the entrance to a room or cupboard and be moved aside to access the space beyond. It is attached to the surrounding architrave by hinges or a rail upon which it slides. Doors are traditionally comprised of several different elements.

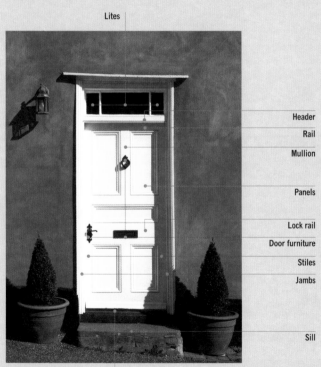

Lites

Header

Rail

Mullion

Panels

Lock rail

Door furniture

Stiles

Jambs

Sill

Threshold

Len Green

Pictured (left) is the Temple of Hephaestus in Athens, Greece, which features Doric columns. Note how they stand directly onto the floor of the temple without a base. Also shown (below) is a detail of a column that has concave grooves in the shaft, a simple rounded capital, and triglyphs, which are placed on the upper half of the entablature.

Andreas Guskos

One of the three orders of classical Greek architecture (along with Corinthian and Ionic). Doric columns stand directly on the flat stylobate or platform surface of a temple, without a base. They have vertical shafts fluted with 20 parallel concave grooves and are topped by a smooth round capital that flares from the column. The Doric order features vertically channelled triglyphs (or decorative blocks), which rest on the plain frieze that occupies the lower half of the entablature.

☞ see Column 87, Corinthian 92, Ionic 143, Orders 187

An Italian term for a cathedral. Derived from the
Latin *domus dei*, meaning house of God.

Illustrated is the façade of Duomo in Milan, Italy. It is one of the largest churches in
the world, and has 135 spires and over 3000 statues. It was commissioned in
1386 and construction did not finish until the early 1800s. It is constructed from
white marble and is magnificently Gothic.

☞ see Gothic 137

Pictured (left) is Salisbury Cathedral; its windows are narrow and lack tracery, which is characteristic of the early English period. Also shown is a view inside the ruined Whitby Abbey (right), another example of the period.

Early English Period (c.1180–1275)
Decorated Period (c.1275–1380)
Perpendicular Period (c.1380–1520)

A style of English architecture that followed the Norman and Romanesque aesthetic and preceded the Decorated Gothic style. Early English architecture is characterised by the pointed arch or lancet that was used for windows and doors. Lancet windows are narrow and lack tracery. In addition to looking elegant, lancet arches efficiently distribute the weight of the stonework resting upon it. The early English style also features high walls and vaulted stone roofs, often given additional support from flying buttresses.

☞ see Decorated Period 95, Perpendicular Period 198

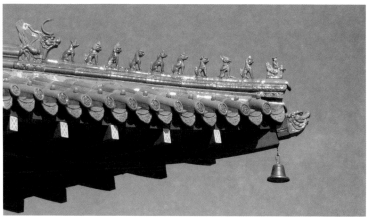

Feng Yu

Aaron Kohr

The under part of a roof's overhanging element, the eaves extend beyond the side of the building. They throw water away from the walls of the building, provide a protected corridor around the structure and form a decorative edge to the roof.

American Craftsmen Style
This style became popular at the end of the nineteenth century and remained so until the 1930s. The style features extensive overhanging eaves, exposed rafters or decorative brackets and a front porch underneath the extension to the main roof. Craftsman (or California) bungalows (left), were built with very wide eaves and decorative brackets.

Khirman Vladimir

The use of many theories, styles or concepts to generate an idea. Eclecticism in architecture sees the use of different historic styles in a single building, an approach popular throughout the nineteenth century.

Pictured is the Duomo di Mantova in Mantua, Italy, which has been successively rebuilt, each time in the style of the period of the day. It therefore exhibits an eclectic architectural mix: a classical façade and bell tower, combined with a baroque interior, Gothic side walls and a Renaissance rose window.

☞ see Architectural Styles 43, Duomo 101

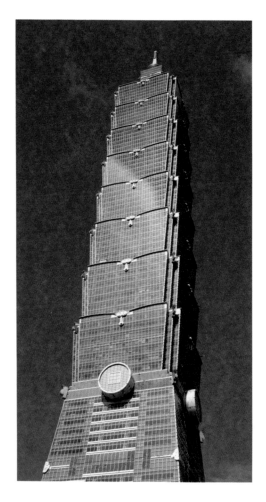

A permanent building or structure with an imposing appearance or size. An edifice is similar in meaning to the term 'building', but suggests something grander and much more impressive.

The Taipei 101 Tower in Taiwan, designed by CY Lee and Partners and opened in 2004 (left), can be described as an edifice. It has 101 floors and is 509.2-metres-high.

☞ see Skyscraper 233

Michael Espanol

An architectural style appropriating visual images from Ancient Egypt. Egyptian revival first appeared after Napoleon's expedition to Egypt in 1809 and, because of the connection between the Pharaoh and death and eternity, became a popular style for cemetery structures.

A more modern interpretation of the style can be found in the Luxor Hotel in Las Vegas, USA. Veldon Simpson, an architect well known for the use of overblown and kitsch imagery, designed the hotel. Opened in 1993, the Luxor Hotel is a 107-metre-high, 30-storey black glass pyramid that incorporates a replica of the Great Sphinx of Giza, amongst other Egyptian structures.

An elevation is the exterior wall of a building, and an elevation drawing is a representation of this wall or façade. It is a two-dimensional representation of the façade, showing the position of windows, doors and any other details of the building exterior. It contains no perspective, so things close up and far away are drawn at the same scale. Elevations are commonly used in the decision-making process of an architectural design as they can provide the client and other interested parties with a visualisation of the finished building.

Pictured is an elevation for the Islands Brygge South development in Copenhagen, Denmark created by John Robertson Architects.

Early Renaissance English architecture built during the reign of Queen Elizabeth I (1558–1603). Elizabethan architecture followed Tudor architecture and is characterised by large-mullioned windows and features such as the Dutch gable and geometric Flemish strapwork. Large, square and tall houses were often built with symmetrical towers that evolved from medieval fortifications. These towers were sometimes shaped like an 'E' for Elizabeth.

Coughton Court in Warwickshire, England pictured is a fine example of Elizabethan architecture.

David Hughes

☞ see Gable 126

An early nineteenth-century design movement originating
in France. Empire style sought to represent and solidify
the achievements of Napoleon and the first French
empire (1804–1814) through the appropriation of
symbolism from the Greek and Roman empires.

Pictured is Monumento Nazionale a Vittorio Emanuele II in Rome, Italy. Giuseppe
Sacconi designed it and, although it wasn't completed until 1925, it was intended
as a tribute to Victor Emmanuel II – the first king of a unified Italy.

☞ see Appropriation 38

Laura Frenkel

An outward or convex curve
in the shaft of a column to
counteract the optical illusion
that gives the parallel sides an
inward or concave curvature.
So, the inclusion of an entasis
makes the sides of the columns
appear straight.

see Column 87

Andrea Danti

Architecture developed by an ancient Italian civilisation (11–1BC), which was assimilated into the Roman Empire. Called Etrusci or Tusci by the Romans, the civilisation had three confederacies: the Po valley, Latium and Campania. Due to a lack of access to fine materials, Etruscans built their temples using wood, terracotta and ornaments; stone was used only for the building's foundations. As a result of the fragility of the materials and the desire of the Romans to erase all memory of them, few buildings remain. Accounts from Roman writers state that Etruscan Temples had high podiums upon which sat square buildings with gabled roofs containing three chambers. A terracotta-tiled roof protected the wood and mud brick block walls, while other terracotta fittings protected the beams and joints.

Illustrated is a tomb at the Etruscan Necropolis in Tuscany, Central Italy.

The 1889 Paris Exposition, or *Exposition Universelle*, saw the unveiling of the 81-storey, 324-metre-high Eiffel Tower (below left) as its entrance arch. The engineer Gustave Eiffel designed the brilliantly imaginative tower. Built from 18,038 pieces of structural iron, 2.5 million rivets, and weighing in at 7300 tonnes, the tower is the most visited monument in the world. Thermal expansion of the iron means the tower top may shift away from the sun by up to 18cm and can sway 6–7cm in the wind.

The Expo originated from the French Industrial Exposition of 1844, and was one of 40 worldwide expositions held in the later half of the nineteenth century, to encourage progressive developments in industry, agriculture and technology. Similar events followed such as the 1851 Great Exhibition in London's Crystal Palace (below right), which was the first international exhibition of manufactured products.

The façade is the exterior front plane of a building; it sets the visual tone and contains many of the identifiable architectural features that are typically used to classify architecture. The term comes from the French word meaning 'frontage' or 'face'. The particular style and historic nature of many façades mean that they are protected by building regulations, which forbid alterations. The regulations governing Park Crescent in London, for example, designed by the regency architect John Nash, specify the exact shade of magnolia paint that must be used to maintain the building's historic appearance.

Illustrated is a contemporary façade study (of 1 Seething Lane, London) by John Robertson Architects, which explores how to optimise wall thickness.

☞ see Fascia 114

A plain horizontal band that traditionally forms part of a classical entablature. Facia comes from the Latin term for 'band' or 'door frame'. Nowadays, a fascia covers and protects the rafter and beam-ends, and as such can form part of a façade.

Pictured is a roof under construction. Note the protective fascia boards positioned directly under the roof slates.

Glen Jones

☞ see Façade 113

A house style commonly found in the USA that is
modelled on the style of French châteaux, but uses
incorrect details and proportions, and misuses the
architectural principles that are applied to the design
and construction of a real château. Faux château and its
synonym 'McMansion' are often derogatory terms that
are used to denote large, generic and culturally
ubiquitous houses.

Morgan Mansour

☞ see McMansion 162

A numerical series where each number is the sum of the preceding two numbers in the sequence (i.e. 1, 1, 2, 3, 5, 8, 13, 21, 34 etc.). The Fibonacci series is named after the mathematician Fibonacci, or Leonardo of Pisa, who observed this sequence in the proportions of the natural world. Numbers from the Fibonacci sequence are used in the Golden Section to produce proportionally beautiful dimensional relationships. Swiss architect Le Corbusier developed a scale of architectural proportion based on the human body, which he named Le Modulor. This system features interrelated modular proportions in increments of 27cm and 16cm. It uses the Golden Section ratio with a combination of proportions produced from of the full height of a man, and those produced from the height of the navel.

The illustration below shows how the length of a man with arm extended (226cm) is twice the height of his navel (113cm). The length from the navel to the top of the head is 70cm (27+16+27).

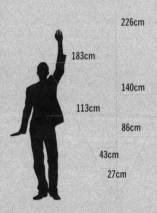

226cm

183cm

140cm

113cm

86cm

43cm

27cm

☞ see Golden Section 136, Le Corbusier 151, Modular 174

Vera Bogaerts

A leaf-line decoration that highlights the apex of a gable.
It can also be found at the top or corner of a building,
bench end or canopy. Straw animals on the ridges of
thatched cottages are also called finials. Finials were
formerly thought to deter witches or flying devils from
landing on the roof.

Oriental pagodas often feature elaborate finials; this detail (above) from a temple at the
Grand Palace in Bangkok, Thailand features a gilded Chofa finial on its roof.

☞ see Canopy 71, Gable 126

A stylised design of the *iris pseudacorus* flower that is used for decorative purposes. The fleur-de-lis ornamentation is particularly prevalent in French architecture due to its symbolic reference to the monarchy. The symbol is believed to have been adopted as a symbol of purity following the conversion of King Clovis I to Christianity in AD493.

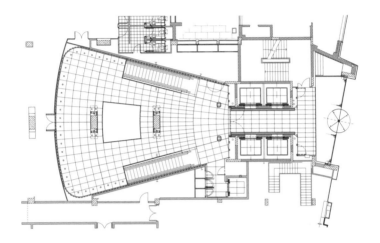

A scale diagram that show the relationships between the rooms, spaces and physical features of a given level of a structure. Floor plans are a horizontal cut through the building, and conventionally provide a view at one metre above the level of the floor. Perspective is not included, so things close up or far away are shown at the same scale.

Pictured is the ground-floor plan of One Knightsbridge Green in London, by John Robertson Architects. The shape of the building is clearly visible, as are the positions of the revolving door, the lifts and the stairs.

☞ see Scale 223

Sir Norman Foster was born in Manchester in 1935. He was a relatively young architect when he designed the highly transparent and controversial Willis, Faber and Dumas Headquarters in Ipswich, England (in 1975). This building, along with the Hong Kong and Shanghai Bank in Hong Kong (1986), put him at the vanguard of international architecture. His modernist high-tech approach is at the forefront of the twenty-first century movement towards sustainable and ecologically sensitive architecture.

The Swiss Re Headquarters in London (right) was designed by Foster + Partners. It is an iconic glass tower with a triangular braced structure, energy conscious glass cladding, solar reflectors and internal gardens that spiral up through the building.

Kevin Britland

There are two types of architectural structure: loadbearing and framed. The loadbearing structure is built up from the ground, brick by brick, while the frame is a skeletal arrangement of struts, ties and beams. The frame has its origins in early tent-like structures and also the trabeated post-and-beam lintel architecture of ancient Greece. The frame, which is usually constructed from steel or reinforced concrete, gives a great deal of freedom in the design of the space. The walls do not have to be connected to the structure and thus the manner in which the space can be used is very flexible.

Illustrated is an example of an A-framed building. The structural shape is exactly like an upper case 'A', with sloping timber sides tied together with a timber cross beam. The structure allows large area of window to be placed on the front and rear façades.

Mark Stout

see House Styles 141, Post-and-lintel Architecture 206

A painting style in which paint is applied to wet plaster. The term comes from the Italian word *affresco* meaning 'fresh'. The technique involves mixing a pigment with water and then painting on wet, fresh, lime mortar or plaster, into which the mixture is absorbed. Frescos are typically luxuriously painted and feature classical, mythical or religious themes.

Frescos typically depict classical, mythological or religious themes. This fresco (above), can be found in in the Collegiate Church of Alquezar, in Huesca, Spain. The fresco from Pompeii, Italy (right), depicts a young male, maybe a god.

Danilo Ascione

A decorated or sculpted horizontal element forming part of an entablature, found above the architrave and below the cornice of a building. Similar to a mural, a frieze adds a decorative element to the top of a building.

Pictured is a frieze of 19 scenes from American history, which can be found on the Capitol Rotunda at the United States Capitol building.

☞ see Architrave 45, Cornice 93

form follows function

A design principle associated with twentieth-century modern architecture that says the shape of a building should be predicated upon its intended purpose. Functionalism, in which form follows function, was popularised by American architect Louis Henri Sullivan. Expressing distaste for architectural ornamentation, functionalists focused on developing plain and simple designs. This enforced the idea that the shape of a structure should be formed by its functional requirements, rather than aesthetics. The building must be fit for purpose.

A gabion is a metal container filled with earth and/or stones. The caged riprap is then used for erosion control and to build dams or foundations. From the Italian word *gabbione*, meaning 'big cage', gabion walls were first developed as a military structure to protect field artillery gunners. Nowadays, gabion walls are used to stabilise shores against erosion and are also used as retaining walls or temporary floodwalls. The gabion is increasingly seen as a viable aesthetic and construction technique for much contemporary architecture.

This gabion wall (below) is used to stabilise a slope or mountain by a road.

Tyler Boyes

The triangular upper section of an exterior wall found between the inclined lines of a sloping roof. The shape of a gable is determined by the structure of the building and its aesthetic styling. The whole wall can sometimes be described as the gable elevation. The gables pictured here also feature decorative exposed rafters.

☞ see Elevation Drawing 107

Guillaume Dubé

A carved stone or wooden fantastical anthropomorphic form. A gargoyle is attached to the rainwater drainage system of a building, usually at roof level, and throws water away from the walls. Gargoyle comes from the French word *gargouille*, meaning 'throat' or 'gullet'. Gargoyles were popular in medieval Europe where they were used on churches as their grotesque forms were believed to scare off evil spirits. However, their use in architecture dates back to the temples of ancient Egypt. Chimeras or grotesques take similar forms, but these figures are only ornamental and do not function as waterspouts.

Pictured is a chimera from the thirteenth-century Galerie des Chimères on Notre Dame in Paris, France.

see Church Elements 79–80

Pictured is Casa Batlló (1905–1907) in Barcelona, Spain, which features skeletal balconies, irregular oval windows, flowing sculpted stonework and an absence of straight lines. Gaudí's masterpiece is the still unfinished Sagrada Família, also in Barcelona, Spain.

Dainis Derics

Antoni Gaudí (1852–1926) was a Spanish modern architect who created beautifully adorned buildings in a unique style. He used gothic and traditional Spanish architectural elements with irregular designs that made use of intricately carved stonework and ceramic tiles. He also created non-linear spaces that appeared to be interwoven with the natural form of the structure.

☞ see Gothic 137

Regina Chayer

A pavilion-type structure that is free-standing, roofed and open on all sides. Gazebos can be made of any building material (such as stone in the example pictured). Gazebos were traditionally placed to take advantage of a view. They were built in many public parks during the Victorian era and were occasionally large enough to serve as bandstands. The gazebo can sometimes be referred to as a 'belvedere'.

Frank Gehry was born in Toronto, Canada in 1929. He developed his unconventional and postmodern architectural approach with the design of his own house in 1978, which is eclectic and takes its style from many different influences and varied materials. However, it is the Guggenheim Museum in Bilbao, Spain (completed in 1997), for which Gehry is renowned. His working method is possibly closer to that of a sculptor – he constructs models from torn and crumpled cardboard, which are assembled and reassembled many times. These models are then translated into architectural drawings through the use of specially developed computer software.

The Guggenheim in Bilbao, Spain (illustrated), is a fine example of Gehry's sculptural approach. Its curved surfaces are clad with titanium sheets and the building appears to be permanently shifting within its dockside location.

The distinctive atmosphere of a location or building. The genius loci is the spirit of a place and the term derives from the protective spirit believed to inhabit a space in Roman mythology. The genius loci may be enhanced through garden landscaping or the effective use of light.

Timur Kulgarin

Stephen Strathdee

An almost spherical structure constructed from a network of struts that are arranged to form the surface of the sphere. The structure is made from geometric elements that have local triangular rigidity and distribute stress across an entire structure or space frame. It is the only man-made structure that gets proportionally stronger as it increases in size. A geodesic dome has the highest ratio of enclosed volume to weight. Buckminster Fuller developed a series of geodesic frame houses in the 1950s and 1960s.

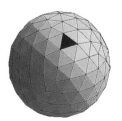

A geodesic dome can be made using either a triangular-based structure (far left) or a hexagonal-based structure (left) as illustrated.

George I
George Louis
1660–1727

George II
George Augustus
1683–1760

George III
George William
Frederick
1738–1820

George IV
George Augustus
Frederick
1762–1830

An architectural style popular in England during the reigns of Kings George I to George IV of Britain. The Georgian architectural saw a return to classical principles of proportion and symmetry. Following on from the English Baroque aesthetic, Georgian architecture featured Palladian and Gothic elements, and is characterised by proportion and balance, the use of simple mathematical ratios to determine the size of different elements, and simple unadorned façades and regular windows.

Illustrated below is the Royal Crescent in Bath, constructed by John Woods the Younger between 1767 and 1774.
The crescent is a series of individual dwellings, but it is intended to be seen as one magnificent edifice.

A highly-decorated style of architecture
from the Victorian era. Gingerbread houses
feature extensive, brightly painted Gothic
woodwork and are so named because they
resemble the witch's house in the fairytale
Hansel and Gretel, a story that was
popularised by the Brothers Grimm in
the early nineteenth century.

see Gothic 137, Victorian Architecture 261

A large steel or iron beam used in construction. Girders are produced in different forms such as an 'I', box, or 'Z' shape. A girder is the main horizontal support of a construction, and it supports the smaller beams. The use of girders in steel-frame buildings allowed for the development of skyscrapers due to their lightweight nature. The building pictured is being constructed with I-beam girders.

Kevin Penhallow

I-beam girder	Box girder	Z-beam girder

Flange

Web

Flange

Flange

Web

Flange

Flange

Web

Flange

Girders are produced in three main forms: the I-beam, which has an I-shaped cross-section; the box girder, which is a hollow rectangular structure with thin walls enclosed on four sides; and a Z-beam, which has an angled profile.

☞ see Steel 242

The approximate 8:13 ratio that was thought by the ancients to represent infallibly beautiful proportions. The Golden Section is used in architecture due to the harmonious proportions it provides, which results in a balanced design.

Constructing a Golden Section

Pictured is the sequence for drawing a Golden Section. Begin with a square (A) and dissect it (B). Then form an isosceles triangle (C) by drawing lines from the bottom corners to the top of the bisecting line. With a compass, extend an arc from the apex of the triangle to the baseline (D) and draw a line perpendicular to the baseline from the point at which the arc intersects it. Complete the rectangle to form the Golden Section (E).

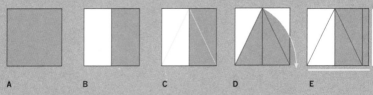

A   B   C   D   E

The principles of the Golden Section can be used to divide a line harmoniously. The line below is divided by the 8:13 proportion. This proportional relationship is at the foundation of the Fibonacci series.

The golden ratio can be applied to any spatial relationship in architecture and has been used by many architects as a means of positioning key elements at focal points. The Golden Section can be used like a slide rule and its use can be seen in examples such as the CN Tower in Toronto, Canada (far left) and the United Nations Building in New York, USA (left).

Guillaume Dubé

Marek Gucwa

An architectural style from medieval Europe that favoured the use of stone to create monumental buildings. The Gothic aesthetic is characterised by the pointed arch, the ribbed vault, clerestory windows and the flying buttress, all of which contribute to a reduction in the width of the walls, the general slenderising of the structure and the formation of a dramatic and splendid architecture.

Notre Dame in Paris, France (above) took nearly 200 years to build and was the first building to use flying buttresses to relieve stress from its high, thin walls. The towers of its western façade have 422 steps leading to the top of the bell tower in which hangs the famous Emmanuel bell. Notre Dame is also known for its four circular rose windows, built in 1250–1260.

Also pictured (below) is the Gothic style interior of Cologne Cathedral in Cologne, Germany.

☞ see Buttress 67, Cathedral 78

Stephen Finn

An architectural movement originating in mid-eighteenth century England, which sought to revive medieval forms in preference to the classical styles prevalent at the time. Popular in Great Britain, Europe and North America, perhaps more Gothic architecture was built during the nineteenth and twentieth centuries than was constructed in the original (medieval) period.

Illustrated is the 98-metre-high Victoria Tower of the Palace of Westminster in London, England. Its architectural style could be referred to as 'perpendicular', which is characterised by long vertical lines and large divided windows. It was built from 1840–70 by Charles Barry and Augustus Welby Pugin. A neoclassical design (similar to that of the US White House and Congress) was avoided due to its revolutionary and republican connotations. The tower holds the parliamentary archives and includes an iron flagstaff from which the Royal Standard or Union Flag is flown.

A garden boundary that was designed to be unseen and therefore provide an uninterrupted view, creating the impression that the garden continued, without disturbance, into the countryside. A ha-ha has a trench or ditch that is faced with stone and turfed on the side furthest from the property. The ha-ha is thought to have been created by English garden designer Charles Bridgeman (1690–1738), and by English architect William Kent (1685–1748). The ha-ha was used with considerable effect in the gardens designed by Lancelot 'Capability' Brown.

A cross-section of a ha-ha showing the incline, retaining wall and grass levels (left).

A double-sided ha-ha border at Melford Hall in Suffolk (below).

Graham Bould

Emily Hagen

A organising system where each element is ranked as subordinate or superior to another element. Hierarchy in architecture works in two ways. The first is the hierarchy present within the physical building – different areas are designed so that they are given more weight or space, a reflection of their importance. The second manner in which hierarchy can work is the visual statement of a building. Certain elements within the building may be given greater visual status, such as a tower, entrance or even a conference room. Within urban design, the site and visual aesthetic of a building may establish its position within the hierarchy of the location.

Pictured is the Cadet Chapel at the United States Air Force Academy near Colorado Springs in Colorado, USA. Designed by Walter Netsch, the 17-spired chapel makes a dramatic statement, particularly given the conservative institution that it represents.

A range of different domestic construction styles that conform to the varying functional needs, material availability, local climatic and environmental conditions and stylistic preferences. House styles are many and varied, but some of the most common are illustrated below.

Cottage
A small, two-storey rural dwelling. The upper level is reduced and restricted by the eaves of the roof that frame it.

Bungalow
A single-storey house. Bungalow derives from the word 'Bengali', and originally meant a house in the Bengal style.

Terrace
A row of identical houses sharing the same side-walls. Terrace housing became popular in England during the Industrial Revolution as they were cheap to produce.

Saltbox
A wood-framed house originating in seventeenth-century New England, USA. This style has a long, pitched roof, flat front and a central chimney. It has one storey at the back and two at the front.

Semi-detached
Pairs of houses built together as a unit, sharing a wall that separates them. The layout of each half mirrors the other.

Detached
A free-standing home built on a site that surrounds it, usually with a garden or yard. Also called single-family home.

Shotgun
A narrow rectangular house popular in the southern USA and comprising three to five rooms in a row without a hallway. Also called a 'railroad apartment'.

Chalet
A wooden building style commonly found in the Alpine region of Europe. Chalets have a sloping roof and overhanging eaves to effectively deal with snowfall.

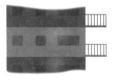

Apartment
A single-room residency, with variations including the L-shaped or 'alcove' studio, where an area is assigned to either sleeping or dining.

A modernist architectural style from the 1920s and 1930s. 'International style' was a term coined by Henry-Russell Hitchcock and Philip Johnson while writing about the International Exhibition of Modern Architecture held in New York City in 1932. The exhibits characterised the expression of volume rather than mass, balance rather than preconceived symmetry, and the expulsion of applied ornament.

Pictured is Farnsworth House, a weekend retreat near Chicago, USA that was designed and built by Ludwig Mies van der Rohe. The ideas of inside/outside and open/closed are explored in this 1400-square-foot steel and glass house that provides expansive views over the vast lawn.

☞ see Mies van der Rohe, Ludwig 168, Modernism 173

Tyler Olson

One of the three orders of classical Greek architecture. The Ionic order emerged in the mid-sixth century BC and features columns that stand on a base, separating the column shaft from the stylobate (or platform). The Ionic column is more slender than its Doric counterpart, and is eight to nine column-diameters tall. The shaft is usually fluted and the column capital has paired scrolling volutes that rest upon it. The volutes are sometimes angled, to project slightly from the corner of the capital, which ensures that they are viewed equally when seen from either the front or the side.

☞ see Corinthian 92, Doric 100

The most important work on Renaissance architecture, *I Quattro Libri dell'Architettura*, was written by Italian architect Andrea Palladio (1508–1580) and published in 1570. *I Quattro Libri dell'Architettura* (*The Four Books of Architecture*) comprise the four illustrated volumes in which Palladio outlined his views about the nature and practice of architecture and the purity and simplicity of the classical style. The books detailed systematic rules on architecture for both appearance and construction of elements such as walls, frames, ceilings, stairs, doors, columns, roofs, details and windows. The books influenced architects such as Inigo Jones, Christopher Wren and Thomas Jefferson.

Pictured is a portrait of Andrea Palladio (top); the frontispiece of the first edition of *I Quattro Libri dell'Architettura* (above); and an illustration from the 1736 English edition of the same book (right).

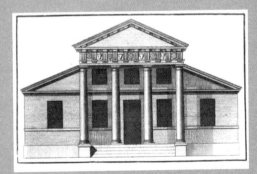

☞ see Palladian 192, Renaissance 216

Jane Sweeney

A gate to the inner city of Assyrian city of Babylon. The Ishtar Gate was built about 575BC by King Nebuchadnezzar II and was one of the Ancient Seven Wonders of the World. The gate is covered with striking blue-glazed tiles and also features bas-relief sirrush dragons and bulls that line the Processional Way passing through the gate. The gate is a reconstruction; only the original foundations and a few glazed bricks were discovered. The reconstructed Gate and Processional Way were built at the Pergamon Museum in Berlin. The structure stands 14-metres-high and 30-metres-wide.

John Said

☞ see Bas-relief 59

Harris Shiffman

A neo-Renaissance architectural style based on sixteenth-century Italian designs. Italianate architecture and first appeared in Britain around 1802 (it was marked by John Nash's development of the Cronkhill country house in Shropshire). The style features low-pitched or flat roofs with projecting eaves supported by corbels, imposing cornices, pedimented windows and doors, tall first-floor windows, angled bay windows, glazed doors, and balconies with Renaissance balustrades.

Pictured is Rengstorff House in Mountain View, California. It features a hip roof with a central gable, crowned by a widow's walk. It has a symmetrical façade with matching bay windows flanking the front door, while a pair of square columns support the portico.

Pictured are a portrait of Inigo Jones by Sir Anthony van Dyck (left); a painting of the Old Palace of Whitehall by Hendrick Danckerts that shows Jones's Banqueting House on the left (top); and Queen's House as it is today with Canary Wharf in the background (above).

Inigo Jones (1573–1652) was the first English architect to study architecture in Italy, where he was much influenced by the work of the great Italian architect Andrea Palladio (1508–1580). Inigo Jones believed that building design should be guided by the principles described by the Roman writer Vitruvius. Jones was the first prominent English architect and his oeuvre includes Queen's House (1616) in Greenwich and Banqueting House in Whitehall (1619), both in London, England.

☞ see Architect 42, Palladian 192

Münchner illustrierte Wochenschrift für Kunst und Leben. — G. Hirth's Verlag in München & Leipzig.

An architectural style similar to Art Nouveau, and prevalent in the late nineteenth and early twentieth century in German-speaking parts of Europe and in Nordic countries. *Jugendstil*, meaning 'youth style', acquired its name from the weekly cultural magazine *Die Jugend*; the front cover of an issue is pictured here, with an illustration by Otto Eckmann.

The style, when practised by architects, is characterised by undulating lines, sinuous curves and the depiction of leaves, flowers and flowing vines combined with austere geometric patterns. The town of Darmstadt in Germany contains many buildings in the style, including the Wedding Tower by Josef Maria Olbrich and houses by Peter Behrens.

An American architect and proponent of the international style, Louis Kahn (1902–1974) produced technically innovative buildings that were highly refined and stylised, such as the Salk Institute for Biological Studies (1959) in La Jolla, California (pictured above). The Salk Institute wanted to form a beautiful campus to attract the world's best researchers, and so Kahn created spaces suffused with light and the sea for both work and contemplation.

Louis Khan's Kimbell Art Museum (pictured above) in Fort Worth, Texas, USA houses a small collection of European, Asian and Pre-Columbian works. The 120,000-square-foot building is a series of spaces defined by parallel barrel vaults given rhythmic variation by interruptions and irregularities. Natural and artificial light is used to enhance the display of objects.

☞ see International Style 142

Voussoirs   Keystone

The central wedge-shaped stone at the top of a masonry arch. A keystone is usually larger than the other wedge-shaped voussoirs or stones that form the arch. This is both for structural and visual reasons. Although the word keystone implies that it is the most important element in the arch, the removal of any voussoir would cause the structure to collapse.

☞ see Arch 41

A leading proponent of the modernist architectural style and one of the most influential twentieth century architects, Le Corbusier (Charles-Edouard Jeanneret) dedicated his life to providing housing solutions for crowded cities. He advanced five points for new architecture published in *L'Architecture Vivante* in 1927. These points were: reinforced concrete stilts (or piloti) to lift the bulk of the structure off the ground; an open plan space that was achieved through the separation of load-bearing columns from the walls; a free façade provided by the open-plan structure; long, horizontal windows that allow unencumbered views of the surroundings; and a roof garden to restore the lost ground area covered by the house.

In addition Le Corbusier developed a scale of architectural proportion called 'Le Modulor', a modular system of interrelated proportions based on the human body and the golden ratio (illustrated below).

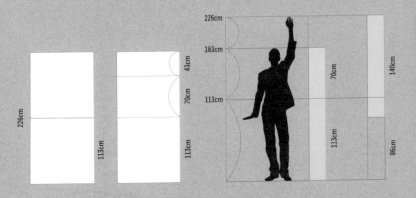

☞ see Golden Section 136, Modernism 173, Modular 174

A horizontal beam made of wood, stone, steel or reinforced concrete that supports masonry above a door or window. Lintels were a prominent feature of Ancient Greek post-and-beam architecture. They are load-bearing and support the weight from the building structure in addition to their own weight. Lintels are often decorated so that they blend in or can actually be hidden within the surrounding structure.

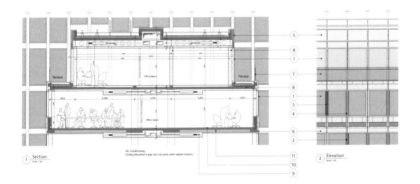

The dynamic load or stress that occurs during the
normal day-to-day operation of a building. The passage
of people in a hallway or staircase is an example of a live
load. When calculating the stresses on a building's
structure, these factors need to be taken into
consideration.

Shown above is a working drawing by John Robertson Architects that illustrates
floor and cladding construction, and also indicates the usage of the building by
showing how it can be occupied and what its suggested live load might be.

An American architect (1867–1959) with a unique
and highly individual style that continues to exert influence
today. Lloyd Wright practised organic architecture
wherein a building was a product of its place and its
time, rather than an imposed style. In this way, he
transformed the maxim of 'form follows function' into
'form and function are one'. This extended to maintaining
a respect for material properties and the harmonious
relationship between form, design and the function of
the building, while attempting to integrate spaces into
a coherent whole.

An example of achieving this balance is the Solomon R. Guggenheim Museum in New
York City (above), which has a dynamic interior space with a spiral ramp. Lloyd Wright's
preoccupation with details extended to the design of the custom-made, purpose-built
furniture and fittings.

An angled slat held within a frame, typically made of wood although other materials can be used. Louvre comes from the French *l'ouvert*, meaning the 'open one'. They are primarily used as window shutters but can also be used for both internal and external doors. Louvres may have horizontal or vertical slats, and function both practically and decoratively. The slats allow light and air to enter a room, and can keep out direct sunlight. As such they are a key element in passive bioclimatic design.

William McCarthy

Inca citadel located high in the Andes Mountains and built around 1460–1470, by the emperor Pachacuti Inca Yupanqui. Machu Picchu comprises 200 buildings that feature cut masonry fixed without mortar. The stone faces were cut so finely and are so beautifully built that a knife cannot be inserted between them. Located between two mountains, the construction of Machu Picchu harnessed the site topography; sculptures were carved into rock, stone channels were cut for water to flow to different cisterns, and temples hanging on steep precipices were created.

Uriel M Ulam

SCOTTISH ARCHITECT AND DESIGNER (1868–1928) WHO WAS PART OF THE ARTS AND CRAFTS AND ART NOUVEAU MOVEMENTS. CHARLES RENNIE MACKINTOSH HAD A STYLE THAT FEATURED THE CONTRAST BETWEEN STRONG RIGHT ANGLES AND FLORAL-INSPIRED DECORATIVE MOTIFS.

PICTURED ARE THE MACKINTOSH ROOM IN THE GLASGOW SCHOOL OF ART (LEFT); AN EXTERIOR VIEW OF THE GLASGOW SCHOOL OF ART (CENTRE); AND HILL HOUSE IN HELENSBURGH, SCOTLAND (RIGHT), WHICH FEATURES A DISTINCT RIGHT-ANGLED LAYOUT WITH CYLINDRICAL TOWER DETAILS.

see Art Nouveau 48, Arts and Crafts Movement 49

An architectural style that emerged after the High Renaissance in the late sixteenth century. Mannerism is characterised by artificial rather than natural qualities, which is typified by the style's elongated proportions. Centred in and around Antwerp, Belgium, Mannerism influenced the Renaissance styles that were introduced into England.

Elongated proportions are evident in 'The Scala Regia' by Hubert Robert (top). The seventeenth century Ducal Mansion (bottom) in the grounds of Nottingham Castle, in Nottingham, England, was built in the Intalianate mannerist style.

Alison Bowden

see Italianate Architecture 146

A Portuguese architectural ornamentation style from the early sixteenth century featuring maritime elements and representations of items brought to the country by explorers from their voyages of discovery. Named after King Manuel I (1495–1521), Manueline (or late Portuguese Gothic) has Spanish, Italian and Flemish influences and features complex ornamentation, often depicting armillary spheres, anchors, and marine elements such as shells, seaweed and columns carved like rope.

Pictured is a crucifixion scene from the Hieronymites Monastery or Jerónimos Monastery in Lisbon, Portugal. Note the Manueline maritime imagery on the columns.

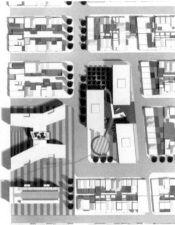

The macro-planning process that seeks to create attractive environments through integrated planning of urban centres. Masterplanning involves the planning of housing, commercial and industrial spaces, green spaces, public spaces and transportation nodes with the aim of developing sustainable communities. The masterplanning process aims to gain the maximum value from site attributes, both natural and man-made, while balancing the needs and demands of various stakeholders. A detailed masterplan ensures that all agreed design components can be positioned within the overall design scheme, with the final result appearing as an aerial snapshot illustrating the proposed layout.

Pictured is the Islands Brygge South development in Copenhagen, Denmark created by John Robertson Architects, in which different areas of the site have been designed by different architects. The masterplan shows how the designs of different architects interact, giving an impression of the final overall result.

Concrete
A pourable material made from Portland cement, sand, gravel, water and admixtures, which harden into a stone-like material. Concrete is often reinforced with steel.

Marble
A cut stone produced from metamorphosed limestone in a variety of colours. Marble is often highly polished to clad buildings for floors and fixtures.

Steel
An alloy of iron and carbon. Often used to produce the frame of skyscrapers and reinforce concrete.

Timber
Sawn wood used for building frames, panels and planking.

Granite
A hard, durable rock used for cut stone and flooring tiles. Granite is available in many colours, and often highly polished.

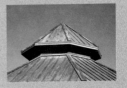

Copper
A non-ferrous metal used for roofing, plumbing, statuary and lighting rods.

Plasterboard
A lightweight panel made from gypsum and often used for interior walls and ceilings.

Glass
A transparent silica-based substrate used to glaze buildings. Fibreglass is also used as insulation.

Brick
A rectangular artificial stone block made with fired clay that is laid in rows with mortar.

☞ see Brickwork 65, Steel 242, Stone 243, Wood 266

Laura Glickstein

A derogatory term from the 1980s referring to large, culturally bland and generic houses that are as ubiquitous as fast-food restaurants. McMansions are characterised by a mishmash of architectural styles all rolled into one building. They may reference classical architecture through the use of columns and porticos, but this could be mixed with the clapboard siding of colonial American architecture. McMansions are typically built with wood-framed stud and plasterboard walls and often feature higher-end surfacing materials such as hardwood, cut stone and ceramic tiling.

At the opposite end of the building spectrum to the McMansion is the Slow Home Movement, a reaction to this style of building, just as Slow Food is a reaction to fast food.

☞ see Faux Château 115

Donald Swartz

A structure built to remember a person or event. Memorials can take many forms, from a cenotaph, to a statue or fountain. Although constructed throughout history, war memorials became increasingly widespread in the twentieth century. For example, of the hundreds of church parishes in the UK, all but a few dozen have war memorials for those killed during the First World War.

Pictured above is the Holocaust Memorial in Berlin, Germany. It was created by architect Peter Eisenman in 2004 and features 2711 concrete slabs in a grid pattern. Also shown is the Vietnam Veterans Memorial (left) by Maya Lin in Washington, USA. The Washington Monument is also visible in the background.

Darryl Sleath

The use of typographical elements in the fabric of
a building to provide specific communication, in addition
to the stories and narratives expressed through
its shape.

Pictured is the Millennium Centre in Cardiff, Wales, designed by Percy Thomas
Partnership. The front face of the theatre shell leans out over the main entrance to the
building and inscribed into it is a statement about the building, the Welsh and their
tradition, by Gwyneth Lewis: *Creu Gwir* In These Stones, *Fel Gwydr* Horizons,
O Ffwrnais Awen Sing.

A device that transfers meaning from one thing to
another, despite the absence of a close relationship
between them. A visual metaphor conveys an impression
that is relatively unfamiliar by drawing a comparison
with something familiar. This can be done directly by
adopting a similar visual form or through the use of
similar materials.

The Sydney Opera House by Jørn Utson, completed in 1973 (top left), creates a visual
metaphor of organic forms such as seashells or waves, which is appropriate given its
harbour location. Another example of an architectural metaphor is the Guggenheim
Museum in Bilbao, Spain by Frank Gehry (bottom left); its form is said to resemble
unfurling tree leaves or spreading roots.

A city with over half a million inhabitants, and at least one million living in its urban agglomeration, which is a major economical, political and cultural centre for a country or region. It comes from the Greek words **meter** meaning 'mother' and **polis** meaning 'city'. Metropolises that are relatively close to one another can form a megalopolis – an extensive metropolitan area or chain of metropolitan areas, such as Rio de Janiero in Brazil.

Pictured is Times Square, located in the megalopolis of New York City, USA.

Alain Couillaud

An intermediate level between any of the main floors of
a building. A mezzanine, or entresol, is not numbered
among the floors of a building, and can take the form
of a balcony.

Randy Piemel

German-American Mies van der Rohe (1886–1969) was a pioneer of modern architecture. Through the use of modern construction materials such as steel and glass, he advanced the international style. His style was encapsulated in such aphorisms as 'God is in the Details' and 'Less is More'. As director of architecture at the Bauhaus, Mies van der Rohe adopted the use of simple geometric forms. After the rise of the Nazi party, he left Germany for the USA in 1937, where his socialist international style became the accepted building model for many for large American corporations.

Pictured is the ivy-covered Illinois Institute of Technology Campus Building, which Mies van der Rohe designed in 1956.

☞   see Bauhaus 60, International Style 142, Minimalism 170

A tall, narrow spire next to an Islamic mosque. The Minaret features a high balcony that is used by the muezzin to make the adhan (call to prayer). A minaret has three main parts: the base, a tapering cylindrical or polygonal shaft that is supported by a spiral staircase, and a gallery or balcony.

This minaret (above) is attached to the sixteenth-century Mosque of Suleyman the Magnificent on the Greek island of Rhodes.

Jeff Banke

less is more

An artistic and architectural style that applies the principles of
Occam's Razor* where the work has been stripped down to its
most fundamental and necessary features. It is architecture that
has eliminated everything but the absolute essentials, and removed
anything that does not coincide with the programme. There is lack
of detail in the connection between planes and an emphasis on the
value of empty space: minimalist architecture is of extreme simplicity
and formal cleanliness. German-American architect Ludwig Mies
van der Rohe (1886–1969) encapsulated the minimalist style in his
aphorism 'Less is More'. Robert Venturi (1925) famously countered the
minimalist maxim with his own aphorism: 'Less is a Bore'.

* Fourteenth-century English logician and Franciscan friar William of Occam is attributed with forming the
principle that is the basis of methodological reductionism: those elements which are not really needed should
be pared back to produce something simple.

☛ see Mies van der Rohe, Ludwig 168

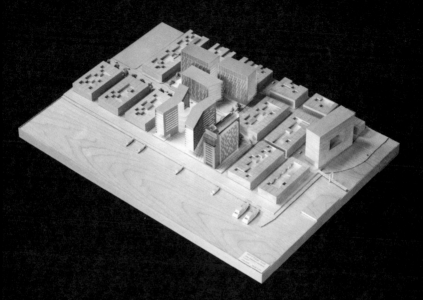

A physical representation of a structure that is used to
communicate design ideas to clients and other
interested parties. A sketch model will aid the architect
in the design of a building, by showing an approximate
three-dimensional representation of it.

Pictured is a model of the Islands Brygge South in Copenhagen, Denmark created by
John Robertson Architects, which provides a three-dimensional explanation of a
proposed project.

Aaron Kohr

The Streamline Moderne style can be seen in the Apartment Block in San Francisco, California (above).

A late development of the Art Deco style (1930–1940) characterised by curving forms, long horizontal lines, and nautical elements (all typical features of passenger liners of the age). Streamline Moderne, which reached its peak in 1937, saw architectural developments using the practical methods, materials, technologies and aesthetics that were employed at the forefront of ship and aircraft development. The resultant buildings were designed so that they actually appeared to be moving.

☞ see Art Deco 47

An art and design movement (1890–1940) that was shaped by the industrialisation and urbanisation of Western society. Modernists, including the Cubist Surrealist, Dadaist, De Stijl, Constructivist, Bauhaus and International movements, departed from the rural and provincial zeitgeist prevalent in the Victorian era, rejecting its values and styles in favour of cosmopolitanism. Functionality and progress, expressed through the maxim of 'form follows function', became key concerns. In architecture, modernism embraced an asymmetrical approach to layout and the abandonment of decoration in favour of geometric forms to create open, functional spaces.

An example of contemporary architecture working in the modernist aesthetic is the America's Cup Pavilion in Valencia, Spain (above). It was completed by David Chipperfield Architects in 2007 and is constructed from overlapping horizontal planes.

☞ see Functionalism 124, Zeitgeist 269

Pictured (above) is the cover of Le Corbusier's Le Modulor. The measurement system he proposed was intended as the basis for determining architectural characteristics based on the proportions of the human body dimensions. For example, 226cm, the reach of an adult male, was intended to be a minimum head height while the 70cm measurement gives seat height.

Standard units or measurements that allow for simpler design and construction. Modular systems can reduce construction time and cost through the incorporation of off-the-shelf components and the selection of standard prefabricated parts.

French, Swiss-born modernist architect Le Corbusier developed his Le Modulor system between 1943 and 1955, proposing a set of coordinated dimensions with which to design architecture based on the body dimensions of a six-foot male. Through this system, Le Corbusier sought to reconcile the physical needs of the human body through the use of two sets of dimensions based on a Golden Section of the height of a man and that of his navel. From this he produced a number sequence from 27cm to 226cm in increments of 27cm and 16cm.

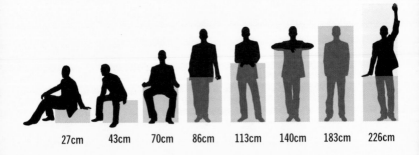

27cm   43cm   70cm   86cm   113cm   140cm   183cm   226cm

☞ see Golden Section 136, Le Corbusier 151

Large-scale architecture that serves an ideological or symbolic function as well as a practical one. Monumentalistic architecture may be built to express religious or political beliefs and convey a sense of the innate power of the builder, such as the three reinforced concrete Kuwait Towers in Kuwait City, Kuwait. The towers were designed and completed by Sune Lindström and Malene Björn in 1979. The main tower is 187-metres-high and houses a restaurant, water tower and a viewing sphere. The smallest, needle-shaped tower controls the flow of electricity to the suburbs in Kuwait, while the middle tower stores up to one million gallons of water.

Islamic architecture erected by the Moors in North Africa and parts of Spain and Portugal between 711–1492. Moorish architecture is characterised by intricate stonework, horseshoe arches and arabesque mosaics and designs.

Pictured is the Alhambra in Granada (left), the seat of the Moorish Kings of Spain and one of the best examples of Moorish architecture. It is a vast complex comprising the Alcazaba or castle, the Palacios Nazaries, and the palace gardens of the Generalife (right).

Sipos András

Adriaan Snaaijer

A design made with small pieces of coloured ceramic, glass, stone or other objects. The tiles can either be exact geometric shapes or created from more haphazard and broken pieces.

Mosaic provides a way to make an attractive, hard-wearing and waterproof surface covering, as can be seen on this bench in Gaudí's Park Güell in Barcelona, Spain. The mosaics were used to help create a wondrous roof-top garden.

☞ see Gaudí 128, Stone 243

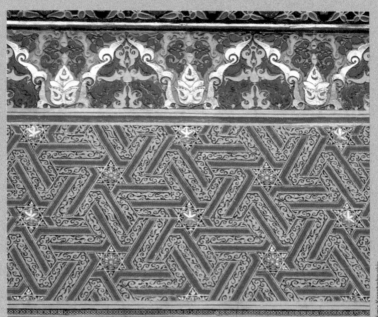

Vladimir Korostyshevskiy

Spanish Christian architecture in the Moorish style that was
popular between the twelfth and sixteenth centuries. It was
highly decorative and fused the Gothic style with Islamic
architectural influences of elaborately worked tiles, bricks, wood
and plaster, incorporating geometric designs that show an
advanced appreciation of mathematics.

Pictured is a detail from the Royal Palace in Aranjuez, Spain.

☞ see Moorish Architecture 176

An English architect from the Picturesque movement who
embraced landscape and urban park design. Nash is best
known for his layout of Regent's Park, Regent Street and
Park Crescent in London. Nash also remodelled
Buckingham House to create the classically inspired
Buckingham Palace (between 1825–1835), and designed
Marble Arch (pictured) in 1828 based on the triumphal
arch of Constantine in Rome, Italy. Originally erected on
The Mall as a gateway to Buckingham Palace, Marble
Arch was moved in 1851 to its present location (at the
western end of Oxford Street, London).

David Burrows

Steffen Löwe

German architecture designed during the period of the country's Third Reich (1933–1945). Architecture played a key role in the attempt by the Nazi party to create a cultural and spiritual rebirth of the country. Lead by architect Albert Speer, Nazi architecture appropriated elements from Ancient Greek and classical Roman architecture. This was combined with an emphasis on the volk (or vernacular) and helped promote Nazi propaganda. The buildings were designed to have a great symbolic quality and to serve a greater purpose than their function. The large-scaled architecture sought to overawe and inspire, and formed part of a victory cult that was complemented by Nazi ceremonial pageantry.

Kehlsteinhaus

Known colloquially as Hitler's tea house or the Eagle's Nest, *Kehlsteinhaus* (left) is a chalet-style building that was an extension of the Obersalzberg complex built by the Nazis in the German Alps near Berchtesgaden.

Kolossron Prora

Designed by Clemens Klotz, and situated in Rugen Island, Germany, these apartments (right) have large windows to allow the access of plenty of fresh air, which was thought to provide a healthy and invigorating environment.

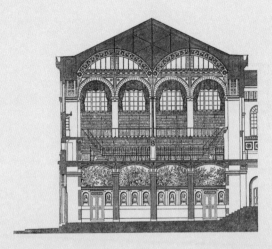

A return to the principles of Greek and Roman architecture. There have been a number of recorded revivals, dating as far back as the eighth century, but it was the rediscovery of the works of Vitruvius in the fifteenth century that allowed a definite theory of classical architecture to emerge.

Andrea Palladio, Inigo Jones and then Christopher Wren were key figures throughout the sixteenth and seventeenth centuries. Étienne-Louis Boullée and Claude Ledoux in France, John Soane in England and Benjamin Latrobe in the USA, all continued the evolution of Neoclassicism during the eighteenth century. The nineteenth and twentieth centuries have seen their own types of revival and the style continues to develop.

Illustrated is a drawing of the Bibliothèque Sainte-Genevieve in Paris, France (1843–1850) by Henri Labrouste. The references to classical architecture can be seen in the use of columns and arches combined with large expanses of window.

A new town is a planned community or city that is designed
and built in a previously unoccupied and undeveloped area.
The entire necessary infrastructure, such as transport
networks, housing, industry and offices, social services,
education institutions and recreational areas are designed as
part of the overall plan, ensuring that all the residents' needs
are provided for. A new town provides an opportunity for the
urban designer to organise the layout of a city in a manner that
will overcome many of the problems that afflict older urban
areas. Ancient cities, for example, particularly those in Europe
dating from the medieval period, suffer from narrow, winding
streets, inadequate services and have difficulty in adapting to
the needs of the twenty-first century.

A well-known new town example is Brasilia, the federal capital of Brazil,
which was built symbolically in the middle of the vast interior of the country.
It was master-planned in the mid 1950s by Lúcio Costa and the plan deliberately
resembles the shape of an aeroplane with its wings outstretched
(as can be seen in the plan pictured above).

A style of architecture from the eleventh and twelfth centuries in northern France and England. It is named after the French Normans who invaded England in 1066, although interestingly, Westminster Abbey was rebuilt in the style by Edward the Confessor between 1050 and 1065. The legacy of Norman architecture is evident particularly in religious and military buildings; the need to quickly erect defences saw the construction of simple, massive buildings with battlements, arrow slits and the round Norman arch positioned over windows and doorways. Following the invasion, nearly every cathedral and abbey church was rebuilt in this style. Norman architecture is the equivalent of what is referred to in Europe as 'Romanesque'.

The White Tower that forms the keep to the Tower of London was built by William the Conqueror between 1078 and 1090. It is set within two parallel rings of defensive walls and a moat. Note the arrow slits in the outer wall, which are characteristic of Norman architecture.

see Castle Elements 76–77

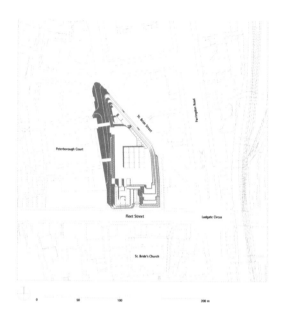

A symbol on a map or architectural drawing showing
the direction of north. The North Point is used to help
orientate the person who is looking at the drawing or map,
and it aids the identification of the exact physical location in
which the building is situated. It is also useful for identifying
such issues as the position of the sun and the shade. It is a
universally recognised symbol and the plan of building
is usually orientated on the drawing so that north point
is facing upwards.

Pictured is a site plan produced by John Robertson Architects. The north point can
be seen within the small symbolic compass on the plan's bottom-left-hand corner.

☞ see Orientation 190

Neil Wigmore

Cowl
A roof element that encourages air movement within the building as it rotates with the wind.

Hot air outlet
An outlet for air escape.

Weather vane
Marks the direction of the wind.

Roundel
Consists of three to four storeys within the body of the building and the roof, for hop drying.

A specialist building developed in south-east England in the eighteenth century for drying hops. Hops were spread over the floor of each of three or four storeys in order to be dried by the hot air produced from a wood or charcoal-fired kiln situated at the at the bottom of the building. The thin, perforated drying floors allowed the heat to pass through and escape via the roof cowl, which pivoted with the wind to allow the kiln fire to draw properly. Oast houses are traditionally circular; their distinctive conical roof is essential to create a good draught for the fire.

🖝 see Rotunda 220

A tall, thin, tapering, stone monument with a rectangular cross-section and pyramidal top. Obelisks have been made since ancient times; they have a symbolic quality and often carry inscriptions. The Ancient Egyptians placed pairs of obelisks at the entrances to their temples to represent Ra (the sun god). Twenty-seven ancient Egyptian obelisks are known to have survived, including a number of the 21-metre-high Cleopatra's Needles, which can now be found in London, Paris and New York City.

Duncan Walker

The two leaning office blocks at the Puerta de Europa in Madrid, Spain (left), flank the monument to Calvo-Sotelo, which is a modern interpretation of an obelisk.

Also pictured are the Washington Monument, USA (bottom left); the red granite obelisk of the Vatican, Rome, which is 25 meters high and weighs 320 tons (bottom centre); and the Luxor obelisk in the Place de la Concorde, Paris, France (bottom right).

Jonathan Larsen

Villedieu Christophe

☞ see Memorial 163, Monumentalism 175

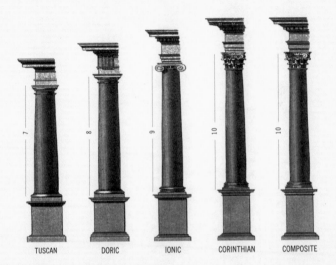

TUSCAN DORIC IONIC CORINTHIAN COMPOSITE

The collection of different elements that together form and define the different styles of classical column. These elements are the base, the shaft, the capital and the entablature. The column (or order) is usually proportioned and decorated in one of five established modes, as illustrated above. The numbers in each illustration refer to the column's height/diameter ratio.

Doric is the oldest order and it comprises a simple vertical tapering cylinder; it generally does not have a detailed capital and often has no base. The most simple order is the Tuscan, and it has cylindrical discs for the base and capital. Its shaft is almost never fluted and it is proportionally slightly smaller and more stout than the Doric column. The Ionic order has a fluted shaft with a volute or scroll-shaped capital. The Corinthian order is characterised by a slender fluted column and an ornate capital decorated with acanthus leaves and scrolls. The Composite combines elements of the Corinthian and Ionic orders. The different orders usually reflected the function of the building that they support, so a cattle shed would generally use the Tuscan, while Corinthian or Composite would be used for a palace.

A fine example of this style of architecture is the Canadian Museum of Civilization in Quebec, Canada. Designed by Douglas J Cardinal, the building responds to the undulating natural shapes of the surrounding landscape.

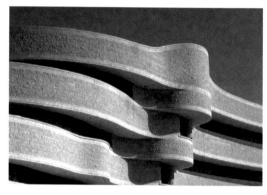

David Lewis

A style of architecture that seeks to harmoniously unify a building with the characteristics of the surrounding site and environment. Organic architecture was a term first used by Frank Lloyd Wright (1868–1959). He declared that decoration should result from the construction rather than be applied to the surface; that the building should be open to allow free movement within and around it; that many geometries should be used rather than just the right angle; that the building should be appropriate to the individual situation; and that the function should be clearly obvious.

The Gaia Charter for Organic Architecture and Design declares that a design should:

Be inspired by nature and be sustainable, healthy, conserving, and diverse.

Unfold, like an organism, from the seed within.

Exist in the 'continuous present' and 'begin again and again'.

Follow the flows and be flexible and adaptable.

Satisfy social, physical, and spiritual needs.

'Grow out of the site' and be unique.

Celebrate the spirit of youth, play and surprise.

Express the rhythm of music and the power of dance.

Lance Bellers

A style of European architecture inspired by Asian architectural forms and popular during the eighteenth and nineteenth centuries, a period that saw great European imperialism in the Asia. Oriental style incorporated features such as bulbous domes, minarets and filigree stonework.

The oriental style is evident in The Royal Pavilion (1815–1821) in Brighton, England (above). It was designed by John Nash and is heavily influenced by Indian architecture.

☞ see Nash, John 179

The specific positioning of a building. Orientation can add significance to a building: it may be designed to catch the sunlight at a precise time of day, or to take advantage of a particular view, or perhaps to respond to its urban environment.

A fine example of how orientation contributes to a building's aesthetic is seen in the Taj Mahal (below). Built on the banks of the Yamuna river in Agra, India, the Taj Mahal is oriented to face the river; it sits on a 50-metre-high platform of red sandstone giving an impression of a cloud-like structure rising from the earth. Completed in 1648, the building is considered the finest example of Mughal funerary architecture incorporating Hindu, Persian and earlier Mughal design influences. The white marble dome is composed of an inner and outer shell that sits on a rectangular podium and is topped by a decorative, gilded finial. A tapering 42-metre minaret stands at each corner of the podium.

Jeremy Edwards

An affectionate term for the multicoloured, gabled Victorian houses built in the Queen Anne style, such as those found in the historic parts of Baltimore, San Francisco and New Orleans in the USA. Although the buildings date from the late nineteenth century, Painted Ladies became a popular expression in the 1970s. Different coloured paint was used to highlight distinct parts of the design and woodwork details.

Pictured (above) are the Painted Ladies on Steiner Street near Alamo Square Park in San Francisco, USA.

Copyright Bill Bertram 2006

A European architectural style that was based on the designs and writings of the Italian architect Andrea Palladio (1508–1580). Palladio practised a style based upon Roman symmetrical planning and classical harmonic proportions. Palladian architecture was prominent from the seventeenth century until the end of the eighteenth century and featured porticos on all sides with façades often modelled on those of Roman temples. Inigo Jones was one of the first exponents of the style in the UK.

Illustrated is Inigo Jones's Queen's House in London, England (left), which was completed in 1635. Note the stark white symmetrical façade with perfectly proportioned windows to walls and the lack of ornament. It would have at the time been thought of as quite shocking. Also illustrated is a drawing from *I Quattro Libri dell'Architettura* (right), which shows the Villa Rotunda (often called the Villa Capra) in Vicenza, Italy, which was designed by Andrea Palladio in 1566.

☞ see *I Quattro Libri dell'Architettura* 144, Jones, Inigo 147

Rome's Panthéon, which was built c. AD125, is a Temple of all the Gods, and can be considered to embody the major creative trends in Roman architecture: the use of traditional classical forms, the development of concrete construction, and the creation of interior space. It is circular in plan, with a rectangular Corinthian portico. The roof is a magnificent dome, constructed in concrete and brick and supported by walls of great thickness. The inner diameter of the dome is 43.2 metres, and is equal to the height of the remarkable space. The interior of the dome is coffered into square compartments. The whole building is lit from a central oculus or opening, an effect that becomes an irresistible climax to every visitor.

Illustrated (below) is the celestial light flowing into the Panthéon's interior via the oculus.

Jeffrey Banke

Blaz Kure

A Greek temple dedicated to Athena and built on the Acropolis in Athens,
Greece in the fifth century BC. The ruins of the Parthenon are one of the
world's great and most recognisable cultural monuments. Commissioned by
Pericles and built by the architect Ictinus, it is considered to be a masterpiece
of the classical Doric order. The Parthenon consists of a stepped platform or
base (the crepidoma), upon which sit the Doric columns that support the
pediment roof. The proportions of the building are based upon the irrational
and divine ratios of the Golden Section. The Parthenon's frieze features a
series of marble panels (or metopes), some of which were removed by Lord
Elgin in 1806 and are now housed in the British Museum in London, England.

☞ **see Golden Section 136**

A means of separating a large open space into smaller, discrete areas. A partition is a non-load-bearing structure that is commonly made from stud wall construction (timber batons faced with plasterboard screens). However, many different materials can be used to create partitions depending upon the amount of separation, levels of visual and aural privacy, and space required. Partitions can be constructed to run the full height of the room or they may just be at shoulder height, providing a certain degree of isolation without cutting off the individual altogether.

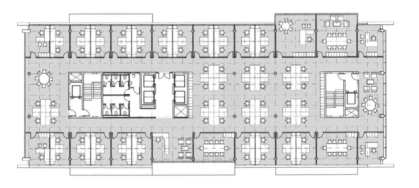

Pictured is a floor plan for an office development by John Robertson Architects. The large, open-plan space has been divided into compartments using a series of partitions that define the meeting rooms, work spaces and circulation routes.

☞ see Floor Plans 119, Materials 161

Jorge Costa

IM Pei was born in China in 1917, but studied architecture in the USA. His buildings are a demonstration of this cultural heritage as he has successfully combined both Asian and European traditions to create buildings that are both sculptural and abstract.

Pictured is Pei's glass pyramid entrance to the Grande Louvre, in Paris, France. Built in 1989, it is uncompromising and effective – it successfully solved the problems of congestion and the lack of service areas without spoiling or overpowering the magnificence of the existing building. The image demonstrates how the new is successfully juxtaposed with the old: the glass pyramid is an iconic statement of modernity, while the original building speaks of classical grandeur.

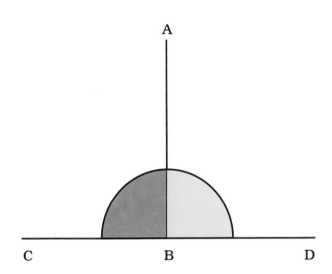

A geometric term that describes an element or line that is at right angles (90 degrees) to a horizontal plane or line. The Perpendicular Gothic style of English architecture is characterised by the emphasis upon the vertical, a devise that encourages the eye to look upwards.

☞ see Perpendicular Period 198

Pictured is the restored fan vaulting in Bath Abbey, England (far left) and an illustration of Westminster Hall by Augustus Charles Pugin (left).

Early English Period (c.1180–1275)
Decorated Period (c.1275–1380)
Perpendicular Period (c.1380–1520)

A division of English Gothic architecture that is characterised by an emphasis on vertical lines. Its aesthetic can be seen in large windows that are subdivided by long slender mullions (or tracery), providing a great canvas for stained-glass designers. The vertical emphasis was further reinforced with wall panels. The supports either side of the window generally extend into the ceiling to become elaborate fan vaulting. The effect is highly dramatic and encourages the eye to move towards the heavens.

Another notable characteristic of perpendicular architecture are the quite extreme hammer beam roofs. During the perpendicular period, advances in joinery and a better understanding of how to distribute the load and thrust of ceiling weight allowed roofs to span great open spaces.

Andre Nantel

Jarno Zarraonandia

Tall buildings that consciously or unconsciously provide a symbolic representation of the phallus. Phallic architecture may take the form of phallic symbols, which were historically used to represent fertility, the male sexual organ and the male orgasm.

An early example of phallic architecture is the Ancient Egyptian obelisk in Istanbul, Turkey (left). It would be naive to label all tall buildings as phallic symbols, but some clearly merit the term, such as the Olympic Stadium in Montreal, Canada (above). Designed by the French architect Roger Tailibert in 1976, it has the world's tallest inclined tower.

☞ see Obelisk 186

A technique where two or more images are combined to create a composite image. For example, the architect or designer may superimpose a drawing of a proposed building onto a photograph of an existing site. This technique is quite easily achievable with CAD software. A photomontage is often used to present views of an unrealised structure to provide a visual representation that potential investors, developers or clients can easily understand. A photomontage should not be confused with a collage wherein an image is formed by combining different media.

Pictured is a composite image of The Daily Express building by John Robertson Architects. The balance of a photomontage rests on both how realistic and how aspirational it is.

A French term that describes the supports used to raise a building to first floor level, thus leaving the ground floor free. Also known as piers, columns, pillars or stilts, piloti are incorporated in many different architectural forms. They provide space below a building that may be used for parking, garden areas or other purposes, and visually lift the enclosed space within its immediate context.

Pictured (left) is the Getty Centre in Los Angeles, USA, which incorporates piloti to great effect. Also pictured (below) is a typical stilt building seen in Castro on the Chilean island of Chiloé. Many such dwellings have a back door that allows people to tie up their boats and enter the building at high tide.

Rodolfo Arpia

Paul Harris

The slope and inclination angle of a roof. The pitch of a roof is measured by expressing the height (or vertical rise) divided by the width (or horizontal span) as a fraction. For example, a three-metre rise over a 12-metre span gives a pitch of ¼. A pitch of less than 15 degrees is classified as a flat roof.

Double or dual-pitch
A standard roof with two equal inclined planes that are separated by a ridge at the top and have a gable at each end (sometimes called a gable roof).

Mono-pitch
A roof with a single inclined plane.

Jarno Zarraonandia

The location in which a building is erected. Place is about more than just a geographic position, it is also concerned with the relationship that is formed between the building and the site that it occupies. Pictured is Euskalduna Bridge in Bilbao, Spain, which was built by Javier Manterola and inaugurated in April 1977. It has been placed near a former industrial site and these qualities are reflected in its design.

Context
This is the built and natural environment within which a building is situated and will form a part. Architecture is often developed to harmonise with the context of the place so that new buildings are woven into the existing fabric of the environment. The Euskalduna Bridge uses an open and massive construction to reflect the industrial heritage of its context.

Site
This is the physical space that a building occupies. The Euskalduna Bridge site is an industrial site in Bilbao, Spain.

Large, prefabricated apartment buildings built during periods of communist party rule and found throughout Eastern and Central Europe. Plattenbau is a German compound of the words *platte* meaning 'slab' and *bau* meaning 'building'. Typically built of prefabricated concrete, plattenbau were cheap and quick to construct.

Tobias Machhaus

☞ see Prefabricated 208

A roofed space that forms the entrance or centrepiece to
a façade. It can be open or closed and is traditionally
composed of columns with a pediment roof. However,
there are many alternative modern interpretations of the
portico form.

The portico entrance to the Chapel of Resurrection in Stockholm, Sweden (left) by
Sigurd Lewerentz is slightly detached from the main building; it is composed of eight
columns with a pediment roof. The portico of St Mark's in Bjorkhagen, Sweden (right),
again by Lewerentz, was designed much later in a modernist style. It too is detached,
but is composed of a broken undulating plane supported by massive double columns.

A construction technique characterised by a horizontal beam that is placed over, and supported by, two vertical posts. Also called post-and-beam or trabeated architecture, this method is commonly used to support windows and doors, in addition to the creation of simple free-standing structures (such as those at Stonehenge in England). Post-and-lintel structures are restricted in the amount of weight they can support, and the length of the beam limits the distance between the two support posts. Such limitations led the Romans to develop the arch.

☞ see Arch 41, Roman Architecture 219

A creative movement (1960–present) that questions the notion of a reliable reality, authority and the established order by engaging in the ideas of fragmentation, incoherence and the plain ridiculous. A reaction to modernism, postmodernism returns to earlier ideas of adornment and decoration, celebrating expression and personal intuition in favour of formula and structure. Postmodernism rejects the boundaries between high and low forms of art and rigid genre distinctions, by instead emphasising pastiche, parody, bricolage, irony and playfulness.

In architecture, postmodernism rejects the international modern style and form, often producing playful and stimulating results using unorthodox and ironic elements in unusual contexts.

Shown here are the Dali Theatre-Museum (left) by the Murcian architect Emilio Pérez Piñero. It is a postmodern structure with egg adornments on the walls. Also pictured is the gigantic sculpture of a West Highland Terrier by Jeff Koons (right), which is located next to the entrance of the Guggenheim Museum in Bilbao, Spain. The sculpture is a postmodern statement constructed entirely from flowers.

☞ see Deconstructivism 94, Modernism 173

A building method in which component parts such as walls, floors or even entire rooms are built off-site and shipped to the construction site for assembly. The use of prefabricated parts saves time and money in the construction process and facilitates construction in difficult environments such as high altitude locations or those with a short building season due to weather or difficult terrain. Prefabricated housing was widely used in Europe following the Second World War as an economic means to meet basic housing needs after much of the original property stock had been destroyed. This method of building saw a resurgence at the beginning of the twenty-first century – increasingly, whole rooms for buildings that contain a series of functional identical activities (such as student housing) are prefabricated.

Pictured is a drawing of a prefabricated construction system for schools for the London County Council created by architect Erno Goldfinger (1902–1987).

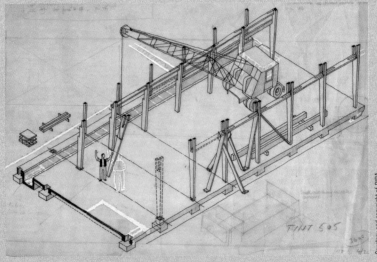

Preferred numbers provide a standard approach to architectural design. This system of 'modular coordination' applies like-for-like dimensions across a series of materials, products and designs.

Major architectural dimensions are expressed as multiples of 100mm, (denoted as 1M). Preference is then given to multiples of 300mm (3M), and 600mm (6M). By designing internal spaces around these measurements, internal fixtures and fittings can be standardised. A kitchen unit, for example, is standardised at 600mm x 600mm (6M x 6M). This means that a kitchen space will have been designed using these dimensions, and therefore any white goods that are allocated to the space will fit. This ensures that all parts of a job homogenise with one another.

Similarly, if you were to buy a pack of screws from one manufacturer and a pack of wall-plugs from another, they will fit together, as both manufacturers will be working to the same set of preferred numbers, as shown below (in the case of screws the preferred number is prefixed with the M designation).

ISO metric thread	M1.6	M2	M2.5	M3	M4	M5	M6	M8	M10	M12	M16	M20	M24	M30	M36	M42	M48	M56	M64
wrench size (mm)	3.2	4	5	5.5	7	8	10	13	17	19	24	30	36	46	55	65	75	85	95

These standard multiples (3M, 6M, 12M, 15M, 30M and 60M) can easily be divided without resulting in awkward fractions. For example, a 6M space can be divided by 2, 3, 4, 5, 6, 8, 10, 12, 15, 20, 24, 25 and 30 and so on without ending up with irregular numbers.

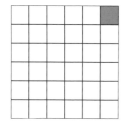

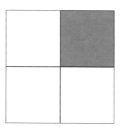

Shown (far left) is a 6M space divided by 6, giving modules of 100mm (1M), and (left) a 6M space divided by 2, giving modular units of 300mm (3M). Importantly, the resulting modules are all whole numbers.

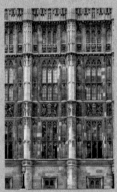

Lance Bellers

A passionate advocate of the Gothic revival style, Augustus Pugin is best remembered for his work on the Houses of Parliament in London, England (above left), for a large number of provincial churches and for authoring a series of influential books on pointed architecture. Pugin worked with Charles Barry on the design for the Houses of Parliament (1840–1868), not just on its Gothic façades, but also the interiors, the fittings and the furniture, and minute details such as hat and ink stands. The building is constructed in the Victorian Perpendicular Gothic style, as is indicated by the emphasis on the vertical and the large divided windows (right).

☞   see Gothic 137, Gothic Revival Architecture 138

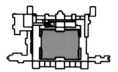

Pictured are a plan of Buckingham Palace, in London with the quadrangle highlighted in red (above). Also a quadrangle of the Sultan Ahmed Mosque in Istanbul, Turkey (below), which is surrounded by richly decorated arcades.

A square or rectangular courtyard that is fully or partially enclosed by the walls of a large building. Quadrangles are formed by the buildings that surround them – it is the building that is deformed or irregular, thus forming square or regular courtyards. Quadrangles are a common feature at many university campuses, and are also typical of much Mediterranean architecture; such houses were built with an inner quadrangle that allowed the marshalling of livestock and some protection from the sun.

Serdar Yagci

☞ see Solar Orientation 236

An architectural style popular in Britain and the USA in the late nineteenth century. The buildings are typically asymmetrical with picturesque detailing such as corner towers, entrance porches, oriel bay windows, white-painted woodwork and fine brickwork finished with terracotta panels or tiles. One of the greatest exponents of the style was Richard Norman Shaw (1831–1912) whose approach to exquisite craftsmanship greatly influenced the Arts and Crafts Movement. In the USA, the Queen Anne Style featured wrap-around porches and vivid colours, which led to the development of buildings colloquially known as 'painted ladies'.

Pictured is a Queen Anne-style mansion in California with a tower, entrance porch and white detailing.

see Arts and Crafts Movement 49, Painted Ladies 191

An early nineteenth century English architectural style that was popularised between 1811–1820 (when King George IV was Prince Regent). Regency architecture is similar to neoclassical Georgian architecture, but has added elegance, featuring column-framed entrances and white-painted stucco facades. Domestic buildings of this period were often built as terraces or crescents and typically included elegant wrought iron balconies and bow windows. John Nash was a great exponent of the style and the houses on Regent's Park Crescent and Lower Regent Street in London (pictured) are fine examples of his work.

Lance Bellers

☞ see Georgian Architecture 133, Nash, John 179, Window 265

Concrete that has been reinforced with steel rods or mesh. Concrete is very strong in compression, but weak in tension and so without the reinforcement it would be too brittle to withstand stress. Reinforced concrete was first developed in 1848, but it was not until 1893 that it was first used in construction (to build the Pacific Coast Borax's refinery in California, USA).

Reinforced concrete is typically used for slabs, walls, beams, columns, foundations, frames and many other building elements. The rods or mesh are placed within the mould or shuttering first and then the concrete is poured in. As the cement hardens it attaches to the textured surface of the steel, which allows the efficient transmission of stress, while the alkaline chemistry of the calcium carbonate in the cement helps protect the steel from corrosion.

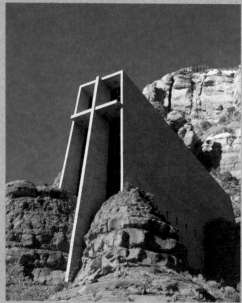

John Blanton

Vladimir Melnik

Buildings erected to serve as gathering places for worship. Religious buildings and structures have driven creative architecture for centuries, from Stonehenge in Wiltshire, England to Notre Dame in Paris France. Religious architecture typically includes symbolic elements and references, such as the orientation of Islamic mosques towards Mecca or cross-shaped Christian churches. Religious architecture may also be elaborately decorated as can be seen in the stained glass windows that are common to many Christian churches or the beautifully embellished domes of many Islamic mosques.

Pictured (above) is the Chapel of the Holy Cross, which is built into the rock cliffs of Arizona, USA. Designed in 1956 by Marguerite Brunswig Staude (who was a pupil of Frank Lloyd Wright), it appears to rise directly from the rock. The Hassan II Mosque in Casablanca, Morocco (left), was designed by Michel Pinseau in 1993. It can accommodate 25,000 worshippers and has the world's tallest minaret.

A term that generally refers to Italian art and architecture from c.1429 to the mid-sixteenth century, a period that saw a revival of learning based on classical sources and the advancement of science.

The word comes from the Italian *rinascimento*, meaning rebirth, and was first used to describe the process of restoring the ancient Roman remains. The Renaissance movement itself was influenced by classical Greek and Roman ideas such as symmetry, proportion and geometry. The return to such classical themes was a popular subject for interior decoration and influenced Italian painters such as Raphael (1843–1520).

Renaissance buildings tend to have a square, symmetrical appearance with central columns and windows, arches supported by piers or columns, decorated flat ceilings and domes.

Pictured is the Basilica Santa Maria del Fiore, in Florence, Italy. The cathedral was designed by Filippo Brunelleschi in 1436 and is a fine example of the style.

The interior of the La Piscine, Musée d'Art et d'Industrie de Roubaix, in Lille, France was remodelled by Jean-Michel Wilmotte in 1996 from a municipal art nouveau swimming pool.

There are a number of different methods used in the conservation of a structure and distinct differences between each approach.

Restoration is the process of returning the condition of the building to its original state. This often involves using materials and techniques of the original period to ensure that the building appears as though it has just been constructed.

Preservation maintains the building in its found state. The building is made safe and any further decay prevented from occurring; the ruined condition will be important to the historical understanding of the place.

Renovation is the practice of renewing and updating a building. The building's function will remain the same and the structure is generally untouched, but the manner in which the building is used will be brought up to date. It is usually the services that require attention.

Remodelling (or adaptation) is the process of wholeheartedly altering a building. The function is the most obvious change, but other alterations may be made to the building itself. Additions or extensions may be constructed, while other areas may be demolished.

The rococo is not a style in its own right, but is the last phase of the baroque. Prominent in early eighteenth-century France, rococo developed from baroque as a reaction to the heavy, opulent aesthetic, and instead was more light, playful and graceful.

Rococo became popular with Louis XV's ascendancy to the French throne and the return of the monarch to the Palace of Versailles. Rococo decoration placed emphasis upon asymmetry, curves and natural forms (such as tree branches, clouds, flowers or seashells), and detailing was frequently highlighted in gold. Rococo rooms were typically rectangular with rounded corners and flat, smooth walls that could be decorated. Woodwork around doors was often carved and the use of mirrors was common.

The grand rococo interior of The Catherine Palace, near St Petersburg, Russia. The palace was the summer residence of the Russian tsars.

Tim Jenner

☞ see Baroque 57

Bartłomiej Kwieciszewski

Roman architecture is essentially based upon the round arch and the dome. It moved away from the more primitive system of post-and-lintel architecture to develop a method of ordered construction that allowed huge, fluid structures to be built. The column became a much-devalued element (and was often used simply for decoration), while the wall became more prominent, which meant that the enclosed area or room became a valued space.

The Colosseum is three levels of arches with an additional solid storey at the top. The columns have very little structural use; they are decoratively attached to the exterior of the walls between the series of identical round arches.

☞ see Classicism 83, Colosseum 86, Post-and-lintel Architecture 206

A building with a circular ground plan and often covered
with a dome. A colonnade will also frequently surround
the room or building. A circular bandstand or gazebo
may also be called a rotunda. The Pantheon in Rome,
Italy is probably the most famous example of a rotunda.

The ceiling of the Texas State Capitol building in Texas, USA was designed by
Elijah E. Myers in 1881. It features the Lone Star state symbol at its centre.

A type of stonework using rough, irregularly shaped or even recycled stone pieces. It is a term that can be applied to several types of masonry construction; rubble can describe the loose stones used as infill between two more regularly constructed walls, or the stones used to construct walls where there has been no attempt to create regular courses; larger stones are used at the base and smaller ones towards the top. Coursed rubble can be used to construct more regular walls. These are often reinforced with mortar or cement. Dry-stone walls are regularly coursed and constructed from carefully selected stones that are bound together through the thickness of the wall by their fit.

Pictured are a detail of a dry-stone wall at St Mary's Church, Batsford, England (above left), which uses rough-shaped stones without mortar; and a close-up of a course random rubble stone wall (above right).

The ruins of this fort (left) have exposed the rubble infill inside the more ordered and finished stone exterior of the wall.

A colonial wooden-framed house with a sloping, pitched roof that originates from New England, USA. A saltbox house is one-storey high at the rear and two at the front, is clad with painted wooden weatherboarding and has shutters at the windows. This house style was popular in the seventeenth and eighteenth centuries and acquired its name from the resemblance to the inlaid wooden box in which salt was stored.

Pictured is the James Johnston House in California, USA. Note its white painted wooden walls and the contrasting dark shutters.

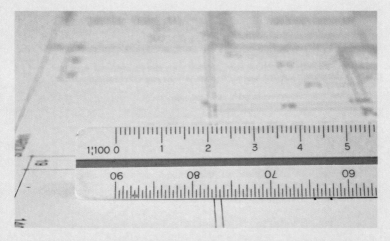

Scale is a method of making comparisons between elements of different sizes. The architect will use scale to calculate the size of a measured drawing of a site, building or object. There will be a direct comparison between the drawing and the finished piece, so if, for example, a building is drawn at a scale of 1:20, the drawing will be 20 times smaller than the building's full size. Certain conventional scales are used on measured drawings, these scales are generally very small for a site map, (such as 1:1250 or 1:2500) and much larger for building design drawings (1:200, 1:100, for example), while details can be drawn at 1:20, 1:5 or 1:1. Very intricate work can be drawn at scales of 2:1 or larger.

Andrey Popov

Sculpture traditionally refers to three-dimensional objects carved from wood or stone, or cast in bronze or iron; however, increasingly a wide range of materials can be used. A sculpture can serve an aesthetic function, providing a visual point of intrigue. It may be placed inside or outside a building and will often serve to complement the architectural form.

Pictured (left) is a detail of Cloud Gate, a highly polished steel sculpture in Millennium Park, Chicago, USA completed by Anish Kapoor in 2004. Notice how the curved surface reflects the surrounding skyscrapers and their colours. Also pictured (below) is the City of Arts and Science building in Valencia, Spain (below), by Santiago Calatrava, which can be described as possessing a sculptural quality.

Jarno Zarraonandia

☞ see **Sculpturesque** 225

Rainer Schmied

A building style in which the elements are, or appear to be, sculpted rather than built. Sculpturesque typically produces free-flowing forms as architects seek to break out from the constraints of standard construction and achieve a very distinct visual aesthetic.

The sculpturesque style is embodied in Gaudí's La Sagrada Família in Barcelona, Spain. Gaudí dedicated forty years to the project until his death in 1926 and worked from his imagination to create the distinctive 18 spindle towers that represent the twelve apostles, the four evangelists, and Mary and Jesus. Gaudí's sculpturesque approach has made it extremely difficult for subsequent architects to complete the project even though CAD has sped up construction.

☞ see Gaudí, Antonio 128

Prefabricated, ready-to-assemble houses, bought via mail order from American retailer Sears Roebuck. Sears catalog homes included everything that was necessary for home construction. Over 100,000 houses were sold between 1908 and 1940. The homes were noted for being sturdy and well-designed, and for including indoor plumbing and central heating.

Pictured are illustrations of some of the many houses in the catalogue. Clockwise from top left:
The Willard (No. 3265), The Elmhurst (No. 3300), The Hillsboro (No. 3308) and the New Haven (No. 3338).

☞ see Prefabricated 208

Michael Smith

An architectural style popular during the Victorian era (1865-1880) that typically combines a rectangular tower with a steep but short mansard roof. The mansard roof crest is often trimmed with iron finials. The exterior façades were built with wood, brick or stone and often included paired columns and sculptured details.

Pictured is a Second Empire building from Charleston in South Carolina, USA.

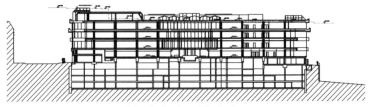

Section drawing of an existing structure

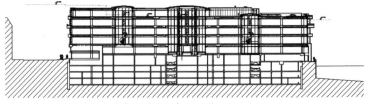

Section drawing of a proposed structure

At any point on the plan of a building, the architect can describe a line through the drawing and represent a vertical cut through of the spaces. This representation drawing is called a section and it explains the volumes of the spaces and indicates the position of the walls, floors, roof and other structural elements. This type of drawing also allows the architect or designer to investigate such issues as the exploration of the structure, the admission of light, vertical interaction within the building and relationships between the interior and the exterior.

Pictured are two section drawings of 10 Queen Street Place, London. The first shows the building as it exists and the second illustrates the proposed changes to be made by John Robertson Architects. The proposed section drawing allows changes to be easily seen.

Architecture of a non-religious nature. Secular
architecture encompasses a wide range of buildings such
as (but not restricted to) houses, palaces, castles,
skyscrapers, gazebos and windmills.

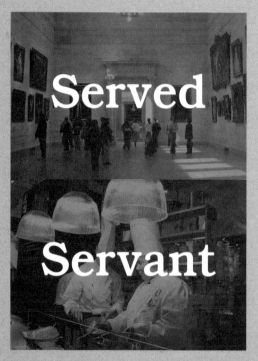

The different types of functional space within a building. As their name suggests, the servant spaces are those which service and support the served spaces. The servant areas include the kitchens, bathrooms, circulation routes, storage and service areas, and heating and ventilation systems. The served spaces are those that are supported, such as domestic living rooms and bedrooms, office spaces and work stations, or retail showrooms. The terms were first coined by American architect Louis Kahn.

see Kahn, Louis 149

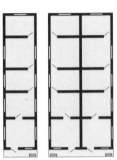

A single shotgun house (left) with an overhanging awning and small porch. The above illustrations show a typical layout of a single shotgun house (on the left) and a double-barrel shotgun house (on the right).

A house style popular in southern USA between 1865–1920 that is characterised by its long and narrow shape. A shotgun house (or railroad apartment), is usually no more than four-metres-wide, and has three, four or five rooms that open on to each other with aligned, interconnecting doors or enfilade organisation. Shotgun houses have front and back doors, but no corridor or hall. They were often built in pairs (these are termed 'double-barrel shotgun houses') and in such instances shared a common central wall, much like today's semi-detached houses.

☞ see House Styles 141

The horizon formed by the profile of city buildings from a viewing point. A skyline can be a very distinguishable feature given that each city is different and the outlines of some buildings are universally recognised. Many cities have planning regulations that control the impact of proposed new buildings on the skyline.

Pictured is an aspect of the London skyline showing Tower Bridge and London's City Hall, which was completed by Foster + Partners in 2002.

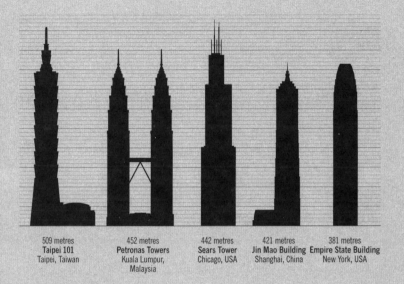

509 metres
Taipei 101
Taipei, Taiwan

452 metres
Petronas Towers
Kuala Lumpur,
Malaysia

442 metres
Sears Tower
Chicago, USA

421 metres
Jin Mao Building
Shanghai, China

381 metres
Empire State Building
New York, USA

A tall, multi-storey building. Skyscrapers are different from towers or masts because they are habitable. The term was first applied during the late-nineteenth century, as the public marvelled at the elevated, steel-frame buildings being erected in Chicago and New York, USA. Modern skyscrapers tend to be constructed from reinforced concrete. As a general rule, a building must be at least 150 metres high to qualify as a skyscraper.

see Reinforced Concrete 214

Pictured are a sod house in the USA, c.1901 (above), and a typical Tequile Island mud home on Lake Titicaca, Peru (top).

A house built from cut sods of thickly rooted prairie grass laid as a masonry wall. Sod houses were built in areas lacking other suitable building materials such as stone and timber. They were usually finished with canvas or plaster on the interior and stucco or wood panels on the exterior. The building method used for sod houses can be applied to other materials, and architects are reprising some of these methods. For example, straw bales give excellent insulation, mud has a beautiful and expressive texture and cob (a mixture of earth and straw) construction is also seeing a revival.

☞ see Materials 161

The underside of an architectural element such as an arch, a flight of stairs, or overhanging eaves. Soffit originates from the Latin word *suffixus*, meaning 'to fix underneath'. The term is often used to refer to the material that bridges the space between the siding on a house and the roofline.

Suzanne Tucker

☞ see Architrave 45

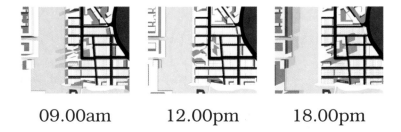

| 09.00am | 12.00pm | 18.00pm |

The location of a building relative to the direction of the sun. The position of the sun is a key consideration when designing a building, as it will influence the nature and quality of the spaces created. Factors such as the direction from which the sun will enter building, natural lighting, the shadows that will be cast and issues of solar gain all need to be considered.

Passive solar design uses non-invasive technologies to maintain a building's environment at a desired temperature (based upon the sun's daily and annual cycles) and thus reduce energy consumption. For example, the amount of direct sunlight entering a building can be reduced, and cooler interiors created, by making use of balconies with deep overhangs.

Pictured above are three diagrams showing the sun path and the extent of the shadows cast for the Islands Brygge South, a development in Copenhagen, Denmark designed by John Robertson Architects.

Antonio Bayesteros

An extreme development of baroque architecture that evolved in Spain and its colonies in the late seventeenth and eighteenth centuries. Spanish baroque featured incredibly elaborate mouldings (generally in white stucco) that were often repeated three or four times, like a series of little pleats, to create a scene of drama and excitement. Described as Churrigueresque after the Churriguera family of Salamanca who were famous for their stucco plasterwork, the work was so sculpturally ornate that for many it bordered upon bad taste. The emergence of the Spanish baroque marked the end of the baroque and rococo periods.

Pictured is a detail of the flamboyant doorway of the Cathedral in Murcia, Spain.

☞ see Baroque 57, Rococo 218

A slender, tall pointed structure rising from a tower or roof. A spire can be conical, polygonal or pyramidal and is usually constructed from stone or timber covered in lead or shingles. It is typically found on a church.

Illustrated is the spire of St Bride's Church in London created by Sir Christopher Wren between 1671–1678. Soon after the spire was completed a local baker used the four-arcaded levels of the bell tower as the model for a wedding cake. This continues to be a popular motif today.

☞ see Wren, Sir Christopher 268

Antonio Iacovelli

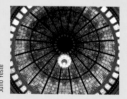

Julio Yeste

Diane Ennis

While stained glass is commonly seen in church windows (left), it is also used to add drama to contemporary architecture, as seen in the dome (above) and wall details (top) pictured here.

Coloured pieces of glass that are held together within a lead frame and form a complete picture. The whole composition is usually held within a window and the arrangement is designed to be read as a narrative or story. The glass used is either stained through the addition of metallic salts during manufacture, or painted and heated in a furnace. Although traditionally found in churches, stained glass is also commonly used in domestic front doors and foyers or entrance areas. The light passing through the glass can be spectacular.

☞ see Materials 161

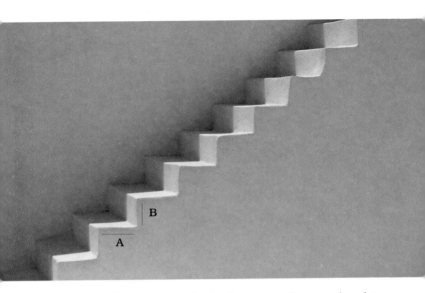

A flight of steps that leads from one floor or level to another. A staircase includes the supporting framework and the balustrade or banister. The tread (A) is the horizontal surface of the stair and the riser (B) is the vertical surface. The nosing is the hardwearing edge fixed at the exposed junction of the two. Triangular steps are called winders, and these are typically found in spiral staircases. The lowest step sometimes has a rounded bullnose to help provide a more stable base for the pickets of a banister and to invite movement.

☞ see Banister 55

A style of architecture prevalent in the Soviet Union from 1933 to 1955. Stalinist architecture, also known as Stalin's empire style or socialist classicism, was architecture on a monumental scale expressing the totalitarian nature of the Soviet regime under Joseph Stalin. Central planning of whole districts saw buildings erected in brick and covered with stucco to impose the presence of the state.

Pictured is the unrealised 1933 design for the Palace of Soviets in Moscow by Boris Iofan.

An extremely hard carbon and iron alloy widely used for construction. The advent of steel revolutionised methods of construction: the steel frame allowed for buildings free from intermediate walls to be realised, and this, coupled with the evolution of steel-reinforced concrete, produced a strong combination that facilitated the development of skyscrapers.

Illustrated is the 38-storey Seagram Building in New York, USA, which was designed by the German architect Ludwig Mies van der Rohe and American architect Philip Johnson. The Seagram is an example of the functionalist aesthetic of the international style and is one of the most influential buildings of the post-war period. It is constructed from a reinforced concrete frame that is clad in a sleek curtain wall, with an exposed bronze structure, and dark-tinted glass.

see Mies van der Rohe, Ludwig 168, International Style 142

St Paul's Cathedral in London was built in 1668 by Sir Christopher Wren. It is constructed from Portland stone, a material that is valued for its pure pale density.

At the beginning of the twenty-first century, stone is a material that is more popular and more widely used than at any time during the previous century. It is a natural material, with inherent texture and warmth. The globalisation of markets means that stone from all over the world is now widely available, and advances in technology have meant that it can be cut or fashioned in ways previously impossible. Architects can incorporate stone traditionally (blocks are cut for load-bearing masonry), but increasingly, it is sliced into thin panels to serve as cladding for buildings.

Robert Gooch

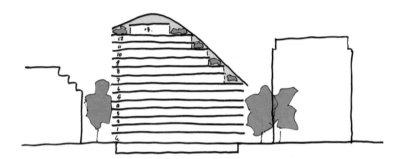

The space between two floors, or floor and roof, of a building. A building that is divided into more than three or four levels is known as a multi-storey building. The height of each storey depends on factors such as the materials used, the function, the location and other aesthetic and physical considerations.

Illustrated is a sectional drawing by John Robertson Architects that clearly shows the division of a building into distinct storeys.

Structure can be described as an assemblage of materials that, when joined together, will withstand the loads and forces to which they are subjected. These loads are not confined just to the weight of the building itself, but will also include such forces as: wind, people, furniture and fittings.

There are two basic methods of construction: load-bearing and frame. The load-bearing structure is thick, heavy and generally constructed from bricks or stone blocks built up from the ground. This type of structure creates small confined spaces due to the restricted span of the roof or floor beams and its windows are of a limited size. The frame structure is constructed from a series of columns and beams, usually organised in a grid formation, which takes the weight of the building. The walls, which take no structural load, can be divorced from the structure and so the choice of cladding material is almost unlimited. This type of organisation is referred to as free-plan.

Picture are a steel-frame structure (left) under construction, and a load-bearing brick wall (above) with insulated cavity.

In architecture, sustainability refers to the use of natural resources in the construction and design in such a way that does not deplete them unnecessarily or wastefully. It also refers to the sourcing and use of construction methods and materials that do not contribute to climate change through either their scarcity or transport to site. All new buildings are expected to observe strict controls on the level of carbon emissions, both during the construction process and over the building's lifetime. Issues of sustainability are becoming central to the development of the built environment.

The Spring Creek Fire Station in Whistler, Canada (left) has a number of energy-efficient features including air recovery units, efficient heating systems and a green roof, which reflects solar gain and acts to insulate the building.

Juha-Pekka Kervinen

Ben Goode

The balance or correspondence of one side of an object, drawing or place with its other side. Symmetry is a feature of classical architecture, where the buildings are typically balanced around a central axis. Symmetry helps achieve an impressive and authoritative appearance, particularly in monumental architecture.

Reflection, **mirror** or **bilateral** symmetry is the most common type of symmetry. It uses an axis or a plane to produce a mirror image.

Glide symmetry is obtained from a reflection that is translated along a line.

Translational symmetry is applied to a group of objects that are the same but are presented in an offset or translational manner rather than being lined up.

☞ see Asymmetry 51

Manfred Steinbach

A Jewish place of religious worship. A synagogue is really a meeting-house rather than a temple, and typically comprises a large hall that is used for prayer and smaller rooms for study. It may also contain a social hall, offices and other rooms. The Torah is read from a large, raised platform or *bimah*; this is also the position that services are conducted from. Synagogue windows are usually curved at the top and squared at the bottom to recall the supposed shape of the Lukhot (Tablets of the Law) that Moses is believed to have received from God at Mount Sinai. Twelve windows may be installed around the main sanctuary to recall the Twelve Tribes of Israel. Typically the Synagogue will adopt the style prevalent at the time it was built.

Vladimir Tatlin's unrealised constructivist tower (his *Monument to the Third International*) was supposed to be erected in Moscow or St. Petersburg after the Bolshevik Revolution of 1917. Tatlin produced sketches and a model for the spiralling tower, which were exhibited in Petrograd in 1920. The model was 670cm high and made from an iron frame resting upon a revolving glass cylinder, but the massive twin-helix sculpture itself was conceived to spiral more than 400 metres high.

Tatlin is credited with being the founder of the constructivism, a movement with an emphasis on abstract architectonic form. The tower was never built – indeed, it is uncertain whether it would have been able to stand up – but the concept was hailed as a symbol of the dynamic nature of the revolution. The intended form suggested revolution and change, while the materials were modern (iron and glass), and therefore represented a severing with the past and the optimism of the future.

☞ see Constructivism 91

Max Alexander

A repeated geometric design that covers a surface without gaps or overlaps. Tessellated patterns are commonly constructed from mosaics of ceramic or glass and generally used for floors and walls to provide a seamless design.

Tessellation is evident on the sea-inspired floor in the foyer of The Daily Express Building in London, England. The building's interior was designed by Robert Atkinson, and the building itself was completed in 1932 by Owen Williams and refurbished in 2001 by John Robertson Architects.

A type of glass used for double-glazed windows that protects against the transfer of sound, heat gain and loss and moisture. Thermopane is used to produce insulated glazing units (IGU) in which two layers of glass are separated by a spacer and sealed to become airtight. The space may be filled with air or an inert gas such as argon or krypton. A partial vacuum may also be created to reduce heat loss from convection and conduction.

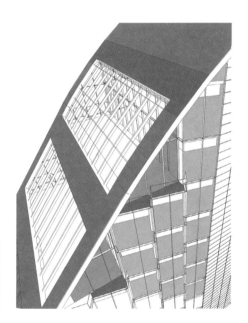

John Robertson Architects

☞ see Window 265

A horizontal bar across a window or panel,
usually constructed from stone or timber. The transom
will divide the window into stages or heights. This
horizontal structure will transfer the dead load of the
glass to the vertical division (the mullion). An external
transom window is typically fixed and does not open,
while internal transoms are often hinged so that they
can provide ventilation.

Troglodyte means cave-dweller, and troglodyte dwellings are therefore caves of holes that are built into or carved out of rock faces.

Humans have carved dwellings from rock in many different cultures. Pictured are a settlement at Chenini in Tunisia (above) and Petra in Jordan (below).

Kirk Geisler

A framework made of a number of timbers that are
joined together to bridge a gap. The truss is most
commonly seen supporting a roof. The triangular roof
truss sits upon, and is supported by, walls or columns at
either end; the sloping sides support the weight of the
roof, while the horizontal member ties the ends together.
The weight of the roof is transferred to the sloping
timbers and subsequently to the walls of the building;
the horizontal timber stops the whole structure from
opening up. The sloping sides are therefore in
compression while the horizontal piece is in tension.
Together they form a strong and stable structure.

Jack Scrivener

English architecture in the early modern historic period (1485–1603) that continued the perpendicular style. Tudor style is characterised by the four-centred or Tudor arch and oriel windows that jut out from the walls.

Mock Tudor describes a revival of the Tudor style, and it became popular in nineteenth-century Britain. The mock Tudor style appropriates elements such as steeply pitched roofs, tall mullioned windows, high chimneys, overhanging first floors and pillared porches.

Pictured is King's College Chapel, in Cambridge, England.

The classification according to general type. Buildings can be classified according to many different variables such as form, shape or the function. For example, a school and a church serve different functions but both could be Victorian or Gothic forms.

Different types of form
Egyptian / Greek / Roman / Byzantine / Norman / Early English / Decorated / Perpendicular / Gothic / Renaissance / Tudor / Elizabethan / Jacobean / Baroque / Queen Anne / Georgian / Rococo / Empire / Regency / Victorian / Italianate / Gothic Revival / Beaux-Arts / Edwardian / Art Nouveau / Bauhaus / Art Deco / International Style / Moderne / Stalinist / Empire / Postmodernist / Deconstructivist / Brutalist / Zoomorphic

Different types of function
Containment / Defensive / Domestic / Entertainment / Food production / Housing / Memorial / Monument / Office / Public building / Recreation / Religious building / Retail / Transportation

A study of the urban environment. Urban design involves the analysis and understanding of the activities that take place within a town. This analysis includes the urban plan and the individual buildings, as well as such issues as topography, history, materials and social issues. The urban designer will typically explore the ideas behind the design of urban space, looking at the influence of politics, ideology and economic forces in the shaping of the city. From this collected information, the urban designer will propose changes to the structure of the city; these will range in scale from small discrete enclaves hidden within the depths of the urban pattern to huge areas of redevelopment.

Picture is the city of Arts and Science building in Valencia, Spain. The concept for this building was to link the centre of the city with the sea.

Vector graphics are scalable systems of image-making, often produced by CAD software packages. Vector graphics were used to produce this illustration for the design of One Great St Helen's in London. The building is shown in relation to other buildings in the vicinity, including the Swiss Re building (right) designed by Foster + Partners.

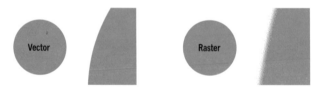

Scalability describes the ability to make images bigger or smaller without the loss of detail or resolution. A vector file enlarged at 500% will show no sign of image degradation; however, a raster file graphic will show a clear loss of image quality upon enlargement.

☞ see CAD 69

Ulrike Hammerich

A type of architecture particular to a given place and time. This style of architecture uses locally available materials and will reflect the environmental, cultural and historical contexts of the location in which it is erected. The wooden barn pictured is an example of the vernacular: it is situated within a heavily forested area of northern Canada. The character of the building reflects the region's climate, the availability of local materials, the surrounding environmental conditions, and its exact position and function.

Mark Bond

A long series of bridges, usually carrying a road or a railway track. Viaducts can be built of brick, iron, steel, concrete or wood, and the material type will determine the span length. The word 'viaduct' is derived from the Latin *via* meaning 'road' and *ductus* meaning 'to conduct something'. Viaducts became a common part of the British landscape in the Victorian era with the development and expansion of the railway and the necessity to connect points at a similar height.

A viaduct should not be confused with an aqueduct, which carries water.

Darryl Sleath

Nineteenth-century architecture developed and built
during the reign of Queen Victoria in Britain
(1837–1901). Victorian architecture is characterised by
large-scale brick and stone buildings with Gothic and
Greek revival influences, which reflect the ambitions of
the Industrial Revolution and the technological
developments of the period.

The Victorian aesthetic is evident in structures such as this red-brick building,
which forms part of the old Welsh Assembly Building (left), and Manchester's town
hall (right).

see Arts and Crafts Movement 49

Structural pigmented glass that is produced by adding fluorides in the firing process, which fuses colour into the body of the glass. Vitrolite was most popular in the 1920s and 30s and was first available in black and white until advances in manufacturing techniques allowed the glass to be pigmented. Vitrolite could be sculptured, laminated, cut, curved, textured and illuminated and it was this versatility that made the glass a firm favourite with designers and architects. Vitrolite's bold colours and shiny, elegant curves were popular in the art deco and art moderne periods, but it ceased manufacture in 1947.

Pictured is the exterior of The Daily Express Building, designed by Owen Williams in 1932, which incorporates Vitrolite glass. The building was refurbished by John Robertson Architects in 2001.

☞ see Art Deco 47, Moderne 172

A drawing by Leonardo da Vinci c.1492, 'The Vitruvian Man' depicts a nude male in two superimposed positions with arms and legs apart, inscribed within a square and a circle. Sometimes called the 'Canon of Proportions' or 'Proportions of Man', it inspired Swiss architect Le Corbusier to develop his modular system of architectural proportion, which he saw as a continuation of Leonardo's Vitruvian Man.

Leonardo made the Vitruvian Man diagram as part of a study of human proportions based on the observations made by Roman architect Vitruvius. He observed that:

A palm = the width of four fingers
A foot = the width of four palms
A cubit = the width of six palms
A man's height = four cubits
A pace = four cubits
The length of a man's outspread arms = his height
The distance from the hairline to the bottom of the chin = one-tenth of a man's height
The distance from the top of the head to the bottom of the chin = one-eighth of a man's height
The maximum width of the shoulders = a quarter of a man's height
The distance from the elbow to the tip of the hand = one-fifth of a man's height
The distance from the elbow to the armpit = one-eighth of a man's height
The length of the hand = one-tenth of a man's height
The distance from the bottom of the chin to the nose = one-third of the length of the head
The distance from the hairline to the eyebrows = one-third of the length of the face
The length of the ear = one-third of the length of the face

☞ see Le Corbusier 151, Modular 174

A spiral, scroll-like ornament commonly found on the
Ionic capital. Smaller versions appear on Composite and
Corinthian capitals. Ionic column capitals are
characterised by four volutes.

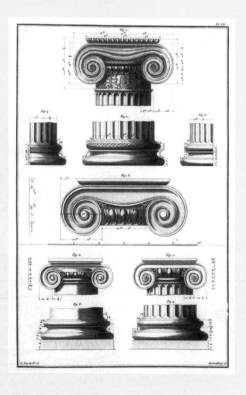

☞ see Composite 88, Corinthian 92, Ionic 143, Orders 187

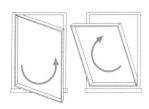

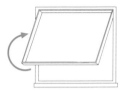

Turn and tilt
A window that turns on its side hinge and also tilts inwards from the top.

Casement
A window hinged at one side so that it swings open vertically, like a door.

Awning
A window hinged at the top so that it opens out and up.

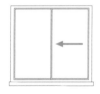

Vertical sash
Window panels that open by sliding in vertical grooves, and use a system of cords and weights for balance.

Horizontal sash
Two or more panels that slide horizontally. The sashes meet and overlap in the middle of the frame.

Hopper
A single panel window that tilts inward.

An opening within a solid surface of a building to light and ventilate an enclosed space. A window is typically made of glass and is held in place by a wooden, aluminium or PVC frame. Windows can be made in many different styles and constructions.

A solid natural material derived from trees. When used as a construction material, it is known as timber. Wood is normally sawn into planks that are then used for the construction of buildings, manufacture of furniture and an array of other uses. Different woods have distinct degrees of hardness, strength, stability and straightness, and produce different visual results due to their colour and grain.

Hardwood
Wood from broad-leaved deciduous trees that typically has high density of hardness and decay resistance; ideal for flooring and furniture. Hardwood is valued for its beauty and texture.

Softwood
Wood from conifer trees: it is easy to work with and is commonly used for making structural elements such as windows and doorframes.

Veneer
A thin slice of hardwood that is applied over a wood or particle-based board to give a decorative finish. This is a cheaper and more environmentally sound option, but not as hard-wearing.

Oak

Walnut

Teak

Maple

Mahogany

Birch

Cherry

Balsa

Cork

The surface of a building that visually encloses it. A
wrapping could be the facia or cladding, and can be
made of many different materials. The wrapping provides
the building with its identity.

Pictured is One Great St Helen's, London. Designed by John Robertson Architects, its
glass wrapping forms a visual as well as a physical enclosure.

Simon Warren

☞ see Fascia 114

Sir Christopher Wren (1632–1723) is considered by many to be the greatest English architect. After the Great Fire of London in 1666, in which four fifths of the city were destroyed, he was appointed as Surveyor General of the King's Works. He was responsible for the rebuilding of St Paul's Cathedral and fifty-one city churches, all in the classical style.

St Paul's Cathedral can be regarded as Wren's masterpiece. It is constructed from the very pale Portland stone and it has a high serene dome above a ring of 32 closely spaced, slender columns. The dome is actually constructed from three domes; the tall upper and decorative lower domes are non-structural, leaving the middle cone to support the two. Baroque influences are evident in the building, most notably in the towers and the main façade.

The moral and intellectual trends of a given era. Taken from the German words *zeit* meaning 'time' and *geist* meaning 'spirit', the term literally means 'the spirit of the age'. The zeitgeist in architecture can be reflected in the choice of materials, colours forms and other stylistic references.

Pictured is Renzo Piano's NeMo (National Centre for Science and Technology) building in Amsterdam, the Netherlands. It is designed as a prow of a ship rising from the bay.

A rectangular stepped tower originating from the
Mesopotamian period. A ziggurat was based upon a
pyramidal shape and usually took the form of a temple
or other place of religious worship. The scale of the
buildings was large and each stage was reached by a
ramp. In the modern age of skyscrapers, the ziggurat has
lost its religious significance, but is still used as a motif
in the designs of buildings (such as the one pictured
above in downtown Texas, USA).

Jarno Zarraonandia

Bill McKelvie

Architecture that echoes animal-like forms or characteristics. Zoomorphism reflects shapes and forms found in the natural world.

An example of zoomorphic architecture is the Clyde Auditorium in Glasgow, Scotland (left), which was completed in 1997 by Foster + Partners. It has overlapping plates or layers similar to that of an armadillo. Pictured (above) is the City of the Arts and Sciences building in Valencia, Spain. Designed by architect Santiago Calatrava in 1998, it is another example of a zoomorphic form.